Simple Pleasures

Simple Pleasures

Little Things That
Make Life Worthwhile

Edited by IVO DAWNAY

National Trust

Published by Random House Books 2010

2 4 6 8 10 9 7 5 3 1

Copyright © The National Trust 2010/individual contributors
Illustrations by Philip Smiley (www.illustrationweb.com)

The National Trust has asserted its right under the Copyright, Designs
and Patents Act, 1988, to be identified as the author of this work

First published in Great Britain in 2010 by
Random House Books
20 Vauxhall Bridge Road
London SW1V 2SA

www.rbooks.co.uk

Addresses for companies within The Random House Group Limited can be found at:
www.randomhouse.co.uk/offices.htm

The Random House Group Limited Reg. No. 954009

A CIP catalogue record for this book
is available from the British Library

ISBN 9781847946416

The Random House Group Limited supports The Forest Stewardship
Council (FSC), the leading international forest certification organisation. All our
titles that are printed on Greenpeace approved FSC certified paper carry the FSC logo.
Our paper procurement policy can be found at www.rbooks.co.uk/environment

Typeset in Sabon MT by Palimpsest Book Production Ltd,
Falkirk, Stirlingshire

Printed and bound in Great Britain by MPG Books Ltd, Bodmin

Contents

PART FIVE:

The Pleasures of the Table

PART SIX:

Talking and Ruminating

PART SEVEN:

Final Thoughts

Foreword

by FIONA REYNOLDS

∼

The deepest pleasures almost always come from the simplest sources.

It is one of the great delusions of our age that we can only find pleasure in ultra-sophisticated, expensive or complex situations. We strive to be in the most glamorous company, to have the latest hi-tech piece of equipment or to be part of the latest fashion.

Yet so often what gives us pleasure comes from the simple reality of nature, architecture, the view, the garden or friends and family enjoying time together. These impulses are a million miles from the illusion that happiness depends on celebrity and wealth. It is so often found in little, usually unremarked things and the cherished places in our lives that evoke comfort, joy and memories as surely as Proust's madeleine.

Walking is my pleasure above all others. The combination of physical exercise and an unfurling, ever-changing landscape taken at a pace one can relish combines a sensory delight with intellectual and spiritual refreshment. Add a map and my joy is complete. Champagne for the muscles and the synapses in equal measure.

So what a delight it is to find in these pages such a diverse range of different and unexpected pleasures, many until now unconsidered and uncelebrated.

The idea of the book came to us at the National Trust when we reflected on what it is we are *really* offering 'for the benefit of the nation', as our statute requires. The words in our founding Act say we exist to *'promote ... places of natural beauty and historic interest'*, but the benefits are not just the places themselves. Of course they are the physical hardware, but they offer so much more.

The real benefits are the experiences people have in those places; what they can offer – anything from a much-loved view to a treasured memory of time well spent with a loved one, family or friends; the experience of being close to nature and the timeless quality of beauty; the joy of freedom from our over-busy lives for a day, or even an hour or two.

As the economic cycle once more switches from the biblical seven years of plenty to seven years of famine, simple pleasures are all the more important: a vital ingredient in the important business of valuing what we have, not regretting what we have not.

This little book is a celebration of things that do not require a lottery win or a banker's bonus to make our lives pleasurable: the sensual, like Patrick Barkham's urban run through rain, Artemis Cooper's morning sunshine or Adam Hart-Davis's working with wood; the delicious, like Zeinab Badawi's apple and blackberry crumble and Prue Leith's whisky and water in a hot bath; animal delights, such as Rosie Boycott's pigs and Roy Hattersley's doggie bedtime; magical places, like Charles Saumarez Smith's Seaton Delaval Hall and Rachel Johnson's Exmoor; activities, from Sally Muir's knitting to Valerie Grove's picking up litter; funny aperçus, such as Lucy Kellaway's cancelled lunch and Mary Killen's joy of cleaning; and sublime and transcendental experiences, from Anthony Seldon's meditation to Matthew Oates's love affair with the Purple Emperor butterfly.

Some of these will surprise you, some will make you laugh, some will make you think. All, we hope, will help to remind you that there are aspects of life – unrecorded in newspapers or on television – that, while so easily left unappreciated, are truly the things that everywhere and every day make our brief lives so worth living.

FIONA REYNOLDS *is Director-General of the National Trust*.

Preliminary Thoughts

The Science of Simplicity

by JAMES LE FANU

There is nothing simple about simple pleasures. The dart of gold of the goldfinch is made more magical still by the billionfold biological complexities of life that sustain it; the delight of a coal fire heightened beyond measure from knowing the warmth of its flames is the consequence of a natural process lost in the aeons of time. These and indeed all simple pleasures act as nodes of amplification of the astonishing in our everyday lives where, in William Blake's immortal lines, it is possible to glimpse 'a world in a grain of sand and a heaven in a wild flower'.

It is the highest purpose of science to deepen our under-standing, the better to appreciate the *extraordinary* concealed behind the ordinary – and no more so than the most recent findings of neuroscience and genetics in revealing the unfathomable profundities of the human mind and the living world.

To start with neuroscience and its implications for the first daily 'fix' of joy on waking: the cherry tree outside my bedroom window. Those bare brown branches silhouetted against the sky will shortly acquire the slightest emerald tinge of springtime buds before being blanketed in the purest, densest, white blossom. Throughout the summer they will remain wrapped in verdant green before transmuting into the reds and golds of autumn, made more iridescent still by the warm glow of early-morning sunshine. Colour – nothing makes the world more beautiful. 'Of all the gifts bestowed upon us,' wrote the Victorian art critic John Ruskin, 'it is the holiest, the most divine, the most solemn.'

And yet, although that kaleidoscope of colours – emerald, white, green, red and gold – seems to be streaming through my bedroom window, they are no more than invisible, weightless, *colourless* subatomic particles impacting on my retina. It is my brain that impresses the colour upon them. 'For the light rays, to speak properly, are not coloured,' wrote the great Isaac Newton in his *Treatise on Opticks*. 'In them there is nothing else than a certain Power and Disposition to stir up a Sensation of this or that Colour.'

More than three centuries on we are still not reconciled to this extraordinary proposition that the world 'out there' in all its vivid and exquisite detail is created within our brains. Until recently the prevailing view held that my cherry tree must (somehow) be impressed on my visual cortex as on a photographic plate. But the sophisticated scanning techniques of contemporary neuroscience have revealed precisely the contrary. Rather, that image, like an exploding firework, fragments in a fraction of a second into thirty or more specialised sites in my visual cortex concerned with the particularities of its colour, movement, shape, position, and so on. There is not the slightest hint here of how their monotonous electrical activity 'translates' into, for example, my subjective awareness of emerald, white, green, red and gold – nor how they are reintegrated back into my unified coherent perception of the tree itself.

'This abiding tendency for attributes such as form, colour and movement to be handled by separate structures in the brain immediately raises the question of how they are all reassembled,' writes David Hubel, past winner of the Nobel Prize for his experimental investigation of vision. 'But where and how – we have no idea.' And that 'no idea' is *no* idea, we no longer have the slightest inkling of the physical basis in our brain of every single, fleeting moment of our lives.

And, moving on from the *mysterium fascinans* – as revealed by neuroscience – of my first glimpse of the cherry tree on waking, there are the equally perplexing insights of modern genetics into the further simple pleasure of visiting the fishmonger and admiring the crab, lobster, squid and oyster, bream, turbot, sole and salmon so elegantly displayed on his counter. Just over twenty years ago when scientists developed the ingenious techniques that would permit them to spell out the full sequence of genes (the genome) of fly and worm, mouse, man and many others, they anticipated, reasonably enough, they would finally understand 'the secret of life' – the genetic instructions that determine the unique characteristics that so readily distinguish one form of life from another.

They were thus more than disconcerted to discover that virtually the reverse is the case – a near equivalence of a modest tally of 20,000 genes across the vast spectrum of complexity from a millimetre-long worm to ourselves. It was similarly disconcerting to discover that the same regulatory genes that cause a fly to be a fly cause humans to be human and that our genomes are virtually interchangeable with those of our fellow vertebrates, such as the mouse and our primate cousins.

So, while the genes determine (as they must) the nuts and bolts of the cells from which all living things are made – hormones, enzymes and proteins of the chemistry of life – the diverse variations of form, shape and attribute that so readily distinguish flies from worms from humans is nowhere to be found. The 'instructions' must be there, of course, for 'life' to reproduce itself with such fidelity from generation to generation, but we have moved in the recent past from supposing we knew the principle, if not the details, to recognising we have no conception of what it might be. And so, too, at the fishmonger. Scientists could, if they so wished, spell out the genomes of crab and oyster, bream, turbot and salmon, but the really interesting question of how and why they are so recognisably distinct from each other would remain as elusive as ever.

It is remarkable the difference it makes to acknowledge that we no longer know (as until recently we thought we might) the nature of those genetic instructions. Suddenly the sheer extraordinariness of that rich diversity of shape and form jostling for attention on the fishmonger's counter – and the florist's and the greengrocer's and the whole glorious panoply of nature – is infused with a deep sense of wonder of 'how can these things be?'

'The world will never starve for want of wonders,' wrote G. K. Chesterton, 'but only for want of wonder.' And we could scarcely be more indebted to the science of the recent past for its revelation of the profundities concealed behind those simple pleasures that reaffirm the 'natural miracle' of our enchanted world. The cherry tree and fishmonger's counter – and my perception of them – are governed by nature and its laws, but their 'true cause' lies so far beyond our comprehension they might as well be miracles.

JAMES LE FANU *is a practising doctor and writes a twice-weekly column for the* Telegraph *newspapers on medicine, science and social policy. His most recent book,* Why Us?: How Science Rediscovered the Mystery of Ourselves, *has just been published in paperback.*

PART ONE

A Sense of Place

The Path to Llangranog

by RICHARD HARRIES

❧

My family roots lie in West Wales and I first walked the coast from New Quay (Ceinewydd) to Llangranog as a boy at the end of the Second World War. At that time it was a very isolated place: I would have to cut my way through ferns and there would be absolutely no one about. I would look down the coast to the wonderful outline of Ynys Lochtyn jutting into the sea and say, as I still say, 'The most beautiful view in Europe.' On the way there is a stream that goes down from Nanternis into the sea, and a short detour up the valley leads to a hidden waterfall that is always magic. A little further up the valley there is the church of St Teilo, set in an ancient pre-Christian circle. Along the coast there are the ditch and banks of an Iron Age settlement. I like to think that my Celtic ancestors lived here, away from the Romans, who did not get this far west. Then, after a break in Cwmtudu and a very steep climb, I would pick my way through the gorse, where there was no path and no right of way, to Llangranog.

For decades this walk was a very personal, private pleasure. It was, as it were, mine, all mine. No one else knew about it. But now, I am glad to say, thanks to the National Trust and others, it has been opened up and others are enjoying it as well. The Ceredigion Coastal Path has just been created, with 60 miles or so from Aberystwyth to Cardigan, complete with stiles and rights of way. If it is good sometimes to walk on one's own, so that one can look at views and think, it is also a great pleasure to share this walk with friends. It is lovely that many others can now enjoy this stretch of coast with more than an occasional sighting of a dolphin, seal or porpoise.

〜 RICHARD HARRIES *was Bishop of Oxford from 1987 to 2006. On his retirement he was made a Life Peer (Lord Harries of Pentregarth). He has written books on a range of subjects – most recently,* Faith in Politics? *and* Questions of Life and Death. *He is a Fellow of the Royal Society of Literature.*

Seaton Delaval Hall

by CHARLES SAUMAREZ SMITH

～

The first time I visited Seaton Delaval was as an under-graduate at Cambridge when I travelled to Scotland in the passenger seat of a small red Triumph Spitfire driven by my friend Adam Bennett, now working for the International Monetary Fund in Washington. We were visiting mausolea in preparation for my undergraduate dissertation. In Volume 11 of H. Avray Tipping's monumental series of volumes published by *Country Life* on English Homes, there is a description of the circumstances which led to the construction of the Seaton Delaval mausoleum:

John, the heir of the Seatons, perished in 1775, having been kicked in a vital organ by a laundry maid to whom he was paying addresses. Thus died the last of the Delavals by the foot of a buxom slut. Over the broken remains of so much hope, the dust of so long glory, his father raised a temple, less to commemorate his achievements than his genealogical significance. The old man stood, last of a dying race, surrounded by childless brothers and sisters, who had, all of them, given happy promise in their youth, and ordered the piling up of cyclopean stones for the reception of the least worthy, but the last of his line. The mausoleum was never consecrated, owing, tradition has it, to the exorbitant fee required by the bishop.

We liked the mock-heroic tone and Gibbonian cadences of this description and the fact that Tipping wrote about architecture as a record of people and historical circumstance, not of architect and design. I only half remember the house from that time, the incongruity and cruelty of its extraordinary landscape setting, close to Newcastle, with the North Sea not far away and the proximity of rough, Northumberland seaside towns.

The second time was driving down from Scotland with my children. We stopped at Seaton Delaval. On this occasion the sun was shining and my children were slightly surprised by my extraordinary and wholly uncharacteristic excitement – in fact, ecstasy – as I jumped out of the car, ignoring passing traffic, in order to take a photograph from the ha-ha by the side of the road. I was inspired by the pleasure of returning to an indisputable architectural masterpiece, looming, hunched, with a restrained sense of potency, now half-ruined, but still powerful, representing so clearly Vanbrugh's response to the north of England and his ability to create blackened poetry in stone. In contrast to so many of Vanbrugh's buildings, not so much is known of the circumstances of its construction or of his relationship to his patron: all that survives is his response to the landscape of the north and his understanding of how to construct an architectural epic on a small scale, packing a punch and demonstrating his resistance late in his career to the smooth, bland correctitude of Palladianism.

The third time was more recently when I took my son and two of his friends, one of whom was studying architectural history at Oxford, on a Vanbrugh tour. We drove to Castle Howard one afternoon in December, long after the end of the visitor season, and were taken out to the mausoleum. The following day we went to Seaton Delaval. We walked around the ruins of the interior and saw once again the nobility of the stables.

In the end, it is architecture which makes my heart beat: the feeling of the manipulation of space in stone. Nobody does it in the same way as John Vanbrugh, the great playwright of architecture. It is not a simple pleasure, but a sophisticated one – so much deeper and more intense than life's more ephemeral pleasures – each generation creating places and spaces and architectural experiences for generations beyond, the still unborn who can experience the resonance of past people in the corridors and staircases and fireplaces left hanging in mid-air by the loss of the intervening floors.

CHARLES SAUMAREZ SMITH *is Secretary and Chief Executive of the Royal Academy and was previously Director of the National Gallery and the National Portrait Gallery. He is the author of* The Building of Castle Howard.

On Exmoor

by RACHEL JOHNSON

On New Year's Day, a woman came to interview me for the *Exmoor Magazine* (keenly recommended for those interested in important subjects like otter spraint and dry-stone walling). It became apparent in the first few minutes that she knew only two things about me: who I was related to and where I lived.

In retaliation, I immediately invited my interviewee to accompany me on a vertical walk up the sheer hill behind our farmhouse, skirting the hidden stone lane called Furze Ball, deep within its ferny combe, on our way to the top of the farm, basking in the winter sun. As we climbed, she further revealed that of those two known facts, only one of them mattered to her and the magazine in question: the second. 'What do you love about Exmoor?' she panted.

By this point we were, I would reckon, about 1,200 feet above sea level. The top of the farm was another 200 or so feet above us, and the highest point on Exmoor, Dunkery Beacon, a few hundred feet above that, topped by its nipple-like cairn at 1,705 feet that can be seen for miles around.

The Exe glistening blackly below was streaming its way

towards the sea; the buzzards were hovering; the smell of bracken mulch and wet sheep fleece and woodsmoke filled the nostrils. I stood with my boots planted firmly on the plump hills and considered. It is a terrible cliché to point out that the best things in life are free, but it struck me that no amount of money, not even the billions it took to save the banks, could buy this.

These sights and sounds and smells, give or take the odd hedge, B-road and pylon, had remained unchanged for hundreds of thousands of years, and were all mine, and yours, for nothing.

So I pondered how to answer her question. I didn't say that it was the privilege of living in a pristine landscape, because I am aware that the upland landscape of Exmoor is a man-made and managed creation, and didn't relish a discussion on this point.

Nor did I particularly want to get into how remarkable and moving it was to be standing on a hilltop in the southwest of England, the most densely populated country in the EU, on a Bank Holiday, and not only not be able to see (forgive the double negatives) another human being, but not see *another house*. All we could see were sheep, deer frozen on hillsides, bracken-clad valleys, stone walls, orangey-brown mud, trees, grass, the tumbledown ruin of the old barn and moorland uplands, for miles and miles around.

It's hard to describe the 360-degree panorama of natural beauty and colour that is spread out before you like a divine gift from the Bristol Channel to Dartmoor, as you stand on an Exmoor hilltop, and I won't attempt to here. But let me reassure you – these are eye-pleasing, soul-nourishing vistas that I am drawn to seek out several times a day. (The house is in a valley; to get views you have to climb hills, and in a National Park anyone is at liberty to do this.)

Like many other secret or celebrated places of outstanding beauty, Exmoor is – thank goodness – miles too far to commute to from London, and an hour from the nearest motorway. As such it frames for the viewer and provides for the resident, incomer, tourist, for everyone and anyone, a timeless, ageless, Englishness that is beyond price.

It's not merely the landscape; the air is clean. There are few or no people. There is no light pollution. Even better – no mobile phone reception, so people talk to you, rather than thumb their BlackBerries. The people eat wheat, and have wild hair and lower blood pressure.

It's hardly changed at all, which as a natural-born conservative I love, but where it has changed, it's been for the better. Village shops, for example, have massively improved, thanks to the loving attention of committed owners, who are prepared to be shopkeepers, laundry agents, head-hunters, postmasters, bankers, shrinks and confessors. There is more local food, and a pride in produce. Our pub is listed in the *Good Food Guide*, and there is a blueberry farm in the heart of Exmoor and hunting at Exford.

But still the landscape remains, blissfully unaltered: steeply wooded cleeves, babbling, peaty rivers, rolling moorland fragrant with heather and dotted with shaggy little ponies, lush green valleys of Arcadian beauty, high hedgerows brimming with wild flowers and foxgloves, and jagged coastline.

I've been here all my life, and this place has given me measureless joy, and it is a place to which I will never be able to record my gratitude and devotion.

As my son put it when I asked him to name three advantages of Exmoor, land of my fathers, rather than going away for our holidays skiing or to Italy or to Thailand, like all his friends appear to at the drop of a hat: 'It's close, we don't have to buy tickets to get there and it's your homeland.'

'So what do you love about Exmoor?' she asked me, as we stood on the hill.

'This,' I said.

RACHEL JOHNSON *is Editor of* The Lady *and author of two novels,* Shire Hell *and* Notting Hell. *She has lived on Exmoor all her life.*

A World Apart

by KATE HUMBLE

Some great friends of my grandmother's had a house at Sutton on Sea on the Lincolnshire coast and as a child I went there with my family several summer holidays in a row.

One year, when I was about six, I got knocked over by a wave; one minute I was crouched in the sand digging up worm casts and the next I was caught up in a swirling confusion of brown water, my ears, eyes and mouth full of salt and sand. I also, perhaps that same year, found a puffin, in perfect condition apart from the fact that it was dead. It was lying like an abandoned toy in the dunes and I picked it up and gazed at it for hours. Growing up next to a properly messy farm, I had spent my childhood accompanied by the chirps of sparrows and the chatter of starlings, but I'd never dreamt a bird could be as exotic as the little feathered Poirot I held in my hand. Where had it come from with its rainbow beak and neat black-and-white plumage? Surely not England, with its brown birds and brown sea.

Both these small yet unforgettable occurrences made me

begin to grasp that there was something mysterious about the sea and it should be treated with the utmost respect. I continued to view it with a combination of fascination and trepidation well into my twenties. Then, during a weekend in Ireland with my husband Ludo, we saw a sign propped against a tree which read 'Come and Try Diving'. Ludo had wanted to learn for years and was already turning the car up the track before I could admit, even to myself, that the idea rendered me blank with terror.

We were greeted by a giant of a man who, seeing me clearly trying to persuade myself that this really was something I wanted to do, said, 'Don't you worry, love, I've been diving since before that Jacques Cousteau. Used to go with a hose and bucket. I'll look after you.' And look after me he did. With my hand gripping his vast paw we walked down a jetty and into the clear, clean waters off the County Mayo coast. Once I realised that I could put my head under the water and both see and breathe and that my lovely Irishman really didn't seem to mind that I was cutting the circulation to his fingers, I started my first foray into a whole new world.

There was something magical about that first transition between air and water – a passing-through-the-back-of-the-wardrobe moment which even now, after several hundred dives, has not diminished. I will never forget the extraordinary colour of the seaweeds and algae; the gem sparkle of the appropriately named jewel anemones; starfish like lost brooches; the purple sheen of the winkle shells; a flounder, perfectly camouflaged on the seabed, with just its two eyes squashed together on the side of its head giving it away. And suddenly I got it. The sea isn't simply the place where our world ends – a steely grey expanse that stretches beyond the horizon, featureless, unreadable, daunting beyond belief. It is a domain beyond our control, inhabited by creatures who can thrive where humans cannot. To spend time under or on the sea is like accepting a privileged invitation.

I have had some of my most memorable, most enjoyable moments with the creatures and birds of our sea: sitting among the puffin burrows on the Isle of May, listening to their strange calls that were surely inspiration for the sound of Dr Who's Tardis; swimming with the world's second biggest fish, a basking shark, off the Isle of Mull and wondering as it swam towards me, mouth agape sieving up plankton, whether it might just swallow me too and not notice; sitting on a tiny boat at the foot of Boreray, the sky above me dark with squadrons of gannets, the waters around me seeming to boil as they dived, arrow-like, in their hundreds, into its depths.

But I still prefer, if I'm absolutely truthful, to be not on or even in the sea, but beside it. Once I made my home in Wales I discovered the Gower Peninsula, surely one of the wildest and most spectacular bits of Britain's coast, with soaring cliffs, expansive beaches and choughs, gorgeous corvids with gloriously tarty red bills and legs, that soar and strut and call their name to each other across the sound of the pounding waves. I have walked here wrapped up against the driving hail beside a furious sea, crashing in a tantrum on the beach and barefoot in the sunshine beneath a cloudless sky, kicking through the lazy shallows. There is no simpler pleasure, no greater joy, I don't think, than to be walking beside the sea with a couple of happy dogs and a sausage sandwich to munch in the dunes.

KATE HUMBLE *is a writer and presenter, whose most recent television credits include* Springwatch, Who Do You Think You Are?, The Frankincense Trail *and* Autumnwatch. *She lives in Wales with her husband, her dog Badger, a hive of bees and various other hoofed, furred and feathered livestock.*

A Copse Near Bath

by JUSTIN WEBB

❧

Their steadfastness is almost a reproach. *Stop rushing around*, they say, *remember where you came from and where you'll end*.

I grew up in the city of Bath. We lived in a grim modern box on the unfashionable side of town. But boy, did we have a view, cascading across the bowl of the city, with trains to catch your eye in the foreground, the crescents in the half distance on the hills where the posh folk lived and above them a fringe of green, the long crest of the opposite hilltop running across the entire length of the vista. I used to sit in my room and drink it in – a lonely childhood, enriched by a loving mother and a room with a view.

I never gave a thought to the trees. But the shapes somehow entered my consciousness and coming back to Bath years later I noticed one day (did I notice it one day or did it just seep in without a time of arrival?) a particular copse, slightly apart from the others on the left side, and it spoke to me: 'I can see your childhood,' it said. 'Your mum lives on in this view.'

There are perhaps ten trees that seem very close together

in a cluster, tall in the middle and gently curving towards the ground at either end. I say ten trees but I really do not know; the distance is great, probably a couple of miles between you the viewer and the subject. They stand there etched against the sky, utterly changeless.

It is a melancholy pleasure, I admit, seeing them now from the sitting room of the house where my mother died. But as other pleasures fade, the trees seem to me to be coming into their own.

For instance: I used to love the rugby ground. It nestles in the centre of the city right next to Pulteney Bridge and the Abbey. When I was young the very sight of it would thrill. Now I go there and cheer but the pleasure catches in the throat. The wear and tear of life, a son with a life-threatening illness, a mother who's gone, bones that ache, the *vicissitudes* interfere.

On the hill there are no vicissitudes. And in my mind at least, no changes. The trees take me back: to that time of life when anything was possible.

∽ JUSTIN WEBB *is one of the presenters of* The Today Programme *on Radio Four. He was, for eight years, the BBC's man in Washington and wrote a book about America entitled* Have a Nice Day!

Lancashire Pride

by CHARLES NEVIN

No Lancastrian asked to nominate a simple pleasure can ever suggest only one. For the Land of the Red Rose, that precious patch bounded by the mighty Mersey, the great glorious northern Lakes and the splendid sheltering Pennines, has too much magic and marvel to make a single choice possible.

This, after all, is the county that has given the world Arkwright's Spinning Jenny, Crompton's Mule, the automatic teamaker and the jelly baby; the county that has inspired such diverse talents as Sigmund Freud (visited Blackpool twice, and was clearly impressed by the Tower), Butch Cassidy (his dad was from Preston), and just about any great comedian you can think of, from George Formby to Eric Morecambe, Les Dawson and Ken Dodd to Peter Kay, Steve Coogan and Victoria Wood. You should also know that Jeanne Moreau's mother was a Tiller Girl from Oldham.

At a pinch, though, I could just about restrict myself to Ten Great Lancastrian Simple Pleasures:

1. The clank of the tram on those sharp, dark and bright autumn Blackpool nights, when the town is at a roar, filled with the sight of the latest of umpteen generations having a gusting, raucous simple good time.

2. An afternoon promenade down Lord Street, Southport. Napoleon III stayed here as a young man and liked it so much that he later had the boulevards of Paris designed just like it.

3. The wind whipping round you down on Liverpool's Pier Head, surrounded by great monuments like the astonishing Liver Building; by memories of great movements of peoples and cultures; and by the buzz of now and promise of the future up in the city ahead of you.

4. To stand at the foot of the arrow-straight drive up to Hoghton Tower, where the young William Shakespeare spent some time in service. Some jealous souls deny this, but where else could he have got his sense of comic timing (see Formby, Morecambe, etc. above)?

5. Waiting for a train at Carnforth Station, setting for the most romantic British film ever made, *Brief Encounter*. Visit the waiting room where Trevor Howard met Celia Johnson, and mind you don't get some grit in your eye.

6. That moment when the succulent aroma of a meat and potato pie is first released into the grateful Red Rose air. (Remember, too, as you unwrap the newspaper, that Lancs gave fish and chips to a grateful world.)

7. A stranger calling you 'Love'.
8. The view of Manchester from atop Libeskind's spectacular Imperial War Museum of the North. Did you know that Charlotte Brontë began writing *Jane Eyre* in a doctor's surgery in Manchester, and that J. K. Rowling got the idea for Harry Potter on a Manchester train?
9. Windermere at sunset.
10. Last, and more deeply personal, the moment when I become part of the happy, happy mass as my home-town team, St Helens, arch practitioners of the fine northern game Rugby League, a thing of grace and fury, score in the last minute to record yet another victory over the old enemy, poor old Wigan.

All that and George Orwell, too. And did I mention that Jane Austen had a cousin from there? She did.

✎ CHARLES NEVIN *is a journalist and author of two books,* Lancashire, Where Women Die of Love, *a paean to the scandalously ignored high romance of his native county; and* The Book of Jacks, *an exploration of our most popular first name. He is currently working on a history of Knowsley Road, the legendary ground of St Helens RLFC.*

In Combe

by ROBERT MCCRUM

Combe is one of those English country words whose onomatopoeic charm magically translates me to a place that time forgot, a source of happiness as crystal-sure as the Pierian spring. *Combe* is an old Celtic, pre-Anglo-Saxon word meaning 'a deep valley'. In the heart of old England, counties like Hampshire, Wiltshire and Dorset abound with *combes*. Here, in the silent folds of downland and moor, a *combe* can be a deep, lush valley with dancing streams, or the craggy intersection of muddy post-road and remote farm track.

There are still some parts of south and south-west England so untouched by the progress of the centuries that you find *combes* defining the limits of ancient settlements. Near Sherborne, where I went to school, there is West Combe, Combe Parva, Combe Magna and – a wonderful tautology that suggests the Anglo-Saxons never really understood the Celtic world they had just overrun – Combe Valley.

But now, when I think of Combe as a place of tranquillity, happiness, ease and contentment, I think of Combe, lost deep in the Berkshire downs, where a very dear family friend keeps a weekend cottage, scarcely an hour from London.

This is no exaggeration. Usually, when country-dwellers say, 'You must come and see us: we're only two hours from London', it's a flat-out lie. You will be well advised to expect a half day's hard driving, probably through horrendous traffic and/or roadworks. In fact, everything to do with the country requires strict translation. 'Near the sea' can mean 'at least an hour's drive to a car park on a cliff'. That old chestnut, 'a stone's throw', becomes 'several miles down the motorway'. My bête noire is 'a hop and a skip from X'. Count on being hopping mad when you arrive, and only too ready to skip it completely.

But not Combe. This obscure scattering of thatched cottages in a hollow of the Berkshire downs really is just an hour from London and, as you take the long single track road snaking down the shady side of Inkpen Beacon, it's as though you feel the centuries falling away behind you.

You pass the ramparts of an Iron Age fort, and then the gibbet on the Beacon, a reminder of the eighteenth century. You twist between hawthorne and wild brambles, and now you're in Civil War Britain. Pass the old church, and you're back in Norman times. Then, in the village itself, there are flinty tracks and beech hedges, and what Orwell in exasperation called the deep, deep sleep of the English countryside.

And then, here you are in a little piece of paradise with

an unspoilt, timeless view of fields, safely grazing sheep and the sound of rooks chattering contentiously in the beech trees overhanging the lane. I have always thought that this corner of old Wessex, Alfred's ancient kingdom, is one of the most authentically English spots in these islands. *Watership Down* is just over the long hill that dominates the village. Stanley Spencer's *Resurrection* mural in Burghclere Church is just off the route from the M4. King Charles fought the battle of Newbury in nearby fields. By the same token, it takes no stretch of the imagination to picture a Celtic Briton coming up the lane towards you, or an Anglo-Saxon warrior fresh from fighting the Danes at Ethandune.

Of course, the dream of Combe is an escape – and a fantasy. The vapour trails high in the summer skies are a reminder of another, more urgent world of emails and hysteria. But none of that can fully contradict the miracle of the English countryside, even in the age of Google Earth and suicide bombers.

❧ ROBERT MCCRUM *is Associate Editor of the* Observer *and the author of* Wodehouse: A Life *and the recently published* Globish: How the English Language Became the World's Language. *He lives in London with his wife and their two daughters.*

Away from It All on Lundy

by ROBERT HARDMAN

❧

Thousands of people have died negotiating their way around this rock (in one year alone – 1896 – the death toll was 300). So it's with a certain sense of triumphalism that you actually jump from the ferry on to Lundy Island in one piece.

Not that your life expectancy goes up much just because you are on dry land, though. To progress 'inland' from the solitary jetty, you have to zigzag up a road that would almost certainly be closed down if it was on the mainland. Actually, 'road' flatters a mile of track which is just wide enough to accommodate a Land Rover. A more accurate term might be 'ledge'. Periodically, bits of it fall off into the sea.

But you have no choice. Lundy is really a green plateau, 3 miles long and half a mile wide, on top of a granite block parked 12 miles off the North Devon coast. It has no sandy beaches. It is surrounded on all sides by unforgiving cliffs and the only way up is along this treacherous path.

Herein lies Lundy's most appealing quality. Where are

the safety railings? Where are the fluorescent bollards, the fences and the warning notices? There are none. Every year, 20,000 people are attracted to a fortress isle so hazardous that it has accounted for at least four plane crashes. Not bad for a place half the size of Richmond Park. Indeed, it is so fraught with danger that it warrants two lighthouses. (The whole of Norfolk has one and Lancashire none.) And yet, it does not carry so much as a solitary 'Danger!' sign, let alone anything to stop people falling off it.

'If you put up railings, people lean over them,' says Derek Green, the manager and de facto lord of this particular isle. 'If they see a precipice, they take care.'

And that's what I love about Lundy. It is an outpost of common sense. People are not treated as morons so they do not behave like morons. The pub/hub/social centre and parliament, the Marisco Tavern, is the only pub in Britain which never closes, but nor does it suffer from rowdiness. After all, drink too much and you might fall off one of those unmarked cliffs.

No one locks their doors because it is a crime-free zone (well, almost; a fishing rod was stolen in 2008). There are no vehicles apart from Derek's Land Rover and a tractor, both of them doubling up as emergency vehicles. None of the twenty-three houses – ranging from a medieval castle and a Georgian manor house to a converted pig sty – has a television.

It's a little slice of the 1950s but with better food and Gore-tex instead of duffle coats. During the summer months, the population can reach the hundreds – an easy-going blend of birdwatchers, campers, daytrippers and rosy-cheeked families straight from the Boden catalogue. In winter, it shrinks to the hardcore two dozen rat race refugees who live and work here permanently, running the farm, the shop and the pub, protecting the wildlife and maintaining the holiday homes which keep the whole place afloat.

Lundy is no longer the private fiefdom it once was in the days of Thomas Benson, a notorious eighteenth-century smuggler and MP. He was followed by the Heaven family, high-minded Victorian sugar barons, and, in turn, by Martin Harman, an eccentric businessman who was prosecuted for introducing his own currency (the puffin) in 1929. Fortunately, when the last of the Harmans died Lundy was bought for the National Trust, who then leased it to the Landmark Trust, the late Sir John Smith's brilliant scheme to rescue endangered old buildings and secure their future by renting them out as holiday homes.

So what is it which lures so many people here? If you want bleakness and cliffs, there are plenty of less awkward places to go. For such a small place, however, it crams in a lot. I doubt that mainland Devon could come up with 1.7 square miles of terra firma with a story to match Lundy's.

For a start, there is the flora and fauna. Lundy not only has Britain's first marine nature reserve but it is also home to the unique (though inedible) Lundy cabbage. The wild goats, deer and sheep are a legacy of wildlife experiments by the Harman family. (They enjoyed less success with an attempt at introducing wallabies.)

The disproportionately huge church is still in use and is particularly popular with bell-ringing tours and gung-ho wedding parties. Built by a clergyman member of the Heaven family, it inspired Lundy's Victorian nickname – 'the Kingdom of Heaven'.

Then there is Benson's Cave, named after a former MP for Barnstaple who ran a lucrative business deporting convicts to the colonies. Many were just dumped on Lundy to work as his slaves. If any visitors dropped in, the poor wretches would be hidden in Benson's Cave until the coast was clear.

Lundy has something else, too, according to many who have found unexpected solace here. Read the visitor books in the various holiday homes and you find recurring references to the calming, contemplative spirit of the place. Some people come here not to walk but to read or to write. In one remote holiday cottage, I counted four bunks and five dictionaries. Some come here to recover from the outside world. In 1944, the Harmans lost their elder son, John, at the Battle of Kohima where he earned a posthumous Victoria Cross. When the family came to erect a memorial, they chose a disused quarry on Lundy where John loved to play as a child. To this day, it is called VC Quarry.

ROBERT HARDMAN *writes for the* Daily Mail *and is the author of* Monarchy – The Royal Family at Work.

Ramsgate Sands

by CLIVE ASLET

❧

Start at Addington Street, higgledy-piggledy and full of pubs. For my money, the view that opens out from the Regency crescent at the end of it – a sweep of sky, pleasure craft bobbing within the protective embrace of Smeaton's harbour wall, a lighthouse, a ferry to provide a cosmopolitan note as it glides out of the port towards Ostend – is one of the best in the world. George IV once left for the Continent from Ramsgate, when he was cross with Dover for supporting his wife – only once, but they commemorated the event with an obelisk, and the harbour has been allowed to call itself 'royal' ever since. It is at the obelisk that the sands start. Frith painted *Ramsgate Sands*; Queen Victoria cannot have allowed the typhoid that she caught at the resort to colour her memory of childhood holidays, because she bought the picture. All human life was there and it still is.

They are wonderful sands, going on for an eternity; or as far as Margate, which is good enough. You can put up a windbreak and spend the day by the bouncy castle, with Peter's Fish Factory and the Belgian bar to provide rations.

I prefer to press on, round the Cubist chalk of the cliff. Not much animate nature to be seen around your toes, beyond tiny, darting translucent fish that can only be spotted by their shadows. But the flints are each one a knobbly Henry Moore sculpture, contrasted with the egg-smooth ovals of chalk used by irrepressible youth for writing love messages on the sea wall.

There is beach cricket at the cove at Dumpton Gap, and beach huts, and a shade-less tattoo than can be seen nearer town. Sheltered, it is its own world on an August afternoon; but another opens up if you walk ten minutes further. For here is the sedate seafront of Broadstairs, where nobody has told the donkey girls or Punch and Judy men that this isn't the 1950s. Ramsgate has Pelosi's and Broadstairs Morelli's, and you should buy an ice cream at one or other of them. But you don't have to spend anything; childhood can be remembered for free.

❧ CLIVE ASLET *is Editor-at-Large of* Country Life *and writes extensively for papers such as the* Daily Telegraph, Daily Mail *and* The Sunday Times. *His books include* Landmarks of Britain *and* The English House.

The Middle of Nowhere

by GILBERT ADAIR

Yes, you grudgingly admit, it could be worse. What could be worse? British Rail. Here you are, in a densely packed compartment early one Sunday evening in September, and a setting sun, as luridly hued as a blood orange, is bobbing alongside you, seemingly just outside your window. It's true that the window itself is far from pristine and the armrest of your seat is scarred by a small but visible gash, like an open wound. Still, the furnishings are cleaner than on many a train you could mention and the compartment is almost too toastily warm.

Such are the thoughts that pop into your head on the train as it continues to speed through the countryside – well, not speed, exactly, this is England after all, but as it chugs along steadily enough to make you believe, touch wood, that on this particular trip you'll have a chance of arriving at Paddington more or less on time.

Your eyes stray. You give your fellow passengers the once-over. Those infants noisily playing Uno with their grandparents. That teenage girl sitting diagonally opposite you, who, with disfiguringly beetled brow, keeps examining her mobile phone, apparently testing every single button on its keypad yet neither making nor receiving a call or text. That hefty fellow reading – ah, now this is interesting. He's reading a paperback so thick as to be practically cubic. You crane to see what it could be. My god, it's a Penguin Classic! *Les Misérables*! That big lunk whom, in all honesty, you wouldn't care to encounter on a dark night (sorry, but it's impossible not to be condescending when fantasising about total strangers) is reading Victor Hugo's *Les Misérables*, a book you yourself have never managed to finish.

How very touching, you think, patronising as ever. Then it strikes you that, of course, if he's reading this novel, this notoriously unreadable novel, it's because he's been to the show. Yes, that must be it. He took his wife to see *Les Miz*, probably more than once, he loved it and he decided not just to buy but actually read the novel. Now he has (you crane again) what looks like ten or twelve pages to go, and you find yourself touched again, yes, sincerely touched, as you imagine his pride and satisfaction, the pride and satisfaction you yourself would feel, on finally turning the very last of its six hundred-odd pages.

Then it happens. The sensation is at first so faint that, were you not an old, long-suffering British Rail hand, you might not even have noticed it. It's not as yet so much a matter of the train slowing down, more a slackening of what one might call its *pulse*, its internal rhythm – doubly internal because it's a rhythm that has long since detached itself from the external world, from the train itself, and lodged inside your head. And so infallible is it, this internal rhythm, you know, you just *know*, that even if the nondescript spectacle that you see directly outside your window – a barbed-wire fence, a field of grazing sheep, a single, lonely carthorse – appears to be receding in the opposite direction at pretty much the same speed as it did just ten minutes ago, the train, as though nodding off, as though actually about to fall asleep, is ever so cautiously, ever so insidiously, decelerating.

Now there can no longer be any doubt. The engine genuinely is slowing down. In just another minute or two its sluggish new speed will have been halved again. And, no more than minutes after that, the train will altogether have ground to a halt who knows why, or for how long, in that mythic realm of the British transport system, the middle of nowhere.

For some, possibly most, of the passengers, this uncharted, unloved middle of nowhere is a hellish limbo, a joyless no man's land, a sort of pastoral purgatory to be released from as soon as is humanly possible. And yet, and yet. Curiously, yet somehow typically, there comes no negative reaction, none at least either visible or audible, from among your fellow travellers. The infants continue playing Uno, the teenage girl pursues her obsessive investigation of her mobile and you would swear the big lunk is actually relieved to be granted a few more precious minutes to finish *Les Miz* before having to pack it away at Paddington.

And you yourself end by sitting back in your seat and musing – how pleasant to be, for once, not in the middle of somewhere.

✍ GILBERT ADAIR *is a novelist, critic, poet, screenwriter and translator, whose most recent book,* And Then There Was No One, *was the third in a trilogy of Agatha Christie pastiches.*

PART TWO

Home and Hearth

A Nice Hot Bath

by PRUE LEITH

Finding a pleasure that is reliable, available all year, cheap, doesn't deplete the world's resources, causes no harm or pain to animals or humans, and won't offend anyone at all is not easy. However, I confidently nominate a nice hot bath. And before someone tells me that it costs 50p to fill a bath and it is a shocking waste of water, can I plead that I don't do it very often and I make up for it in between with very quick showers, which I hate.

There are two versions of this bath indulgence:

Sunday morning, if I'm lucky, goes like this: up early, walk the dog, get lunch on the go, chores done before ten. Then into the bath with *The Archers Omnibus* on the radio, some bubbly smelly stuff in the water and breakfast at my side. Bliss.

Version Two is the bath after anything strenuous like gardening or tennis or riding, or after hours cooking or writing. Nothing like the benison of hot water and the heady smell of perfumed bath oil. And Beethoven's *Pastoral* or Mozart's Horn Concerto No. 4 on full blast. And a long flute of fizz, or a whisky and water. And peanuts, or nuts and raisins, or those little cheesy bikkies on the side.

I think I get the eating-in-the-bath thing from my mother. One of my earliest memories is of her tea tray (silver teapot, Crown Derby cup, lace cloth, shortbread fingers) on a stool by her bath.

She liked company, too. So do I, though not in the bath. That's my territory. Sharing a bath, even with your beloved, means worrying about your lack of sun tan and the wobbly bits round your middle, and there's the question of who gets the tap end and who gets out first. No, I like being brought a drink while hidden under the bubbles and the bringer then sitting on the loo seat for a gossip.

Lying in a bath for hours seems to be a peculiarly female thing. Some women take it further than I do: expensive essential oils, aromatherapy mini-bottles, candles all around, even rose petals in the water. Like some kind of sacred rite.

But few men lie in the bath. Which is why baths are mostly so badly designed. All bath designers seem to be men, and I wonder how many of them test them for comfort? I've become something of an expert since I'm trying to find a bath for my barn conversion which one day will be, I hope, my retirement home. There are almost no baths with a good wide edge for the gin and tonic, novel, magazine or radio, never mind such basics as soap, loofah, bubble bath and nailbrush. If you buy one of those pretty free-standing baths you will have to put a table next to it. Which you will struggle to reach over the ridiculously high sides of the bath.

I admit my search is complicated by the fact that I want a shallowish bath so that when my legs and arms hardly work at all I will still be able to get out of it. All the free-standing, good-looking baths are so deep I can barely get out of them now. And most of them, because of their depth, have steeply sloping ends so that lying down is impossible. I want a gentle incline so I can lie back, and low enough sides so I can rest my elbows on the rim with my hands comfortably holding a book.

I want to be able to reach the taps without sitting up so I can keep the water topped up (yes I know, more wicked waste), and I'd like the bath to be made of some sort of material that keeps the water insulated and hot.

Oh, and the bathroom should have a view. My present one has reaches of changing sky and the branches of waving sequoias with pigeons on the tippy tops posing like angels on a Christmas tree. It's great.

PRUE LEITH is a cook, businesswoman and writer. She has recently published her fifth novel, A Serving of Scandal, *a tale about love and politics.*

Music

by CAROL ANN DUFFY

Do you think they cried, the children
who followed the Piper, when the rock
closed behind them for ever, or cried never,
happy to dance to his tune, lost
in the music?
And the lame boy,
pressing his ear to locked stone
to carry an echo home in his head,
did he weep, alone, the melody gone? Tell me

who wouldn't toss a coin in a hat
for the busker on blues harmonica, blowing
in the wind;
or stop in the square
by the students there, new violins
gleaming under their chins, the Bach Double
applauded by pigeons;
or smile at the ragged choir
rattling their tins? What's music

the food of? Who hasn't, once, sent over a beer
for the piano player to play it again . . .

a child's hands
on the keys, opening a scale
like a toy of sound; the joy Mozart found
between C and G;
Beethoven leaving his grief in minims,
moonlight, broken chords . . .
and who doesn't lift the lid
and pick at a tune with their fingertip –
Perfect Day, Halleluia, Für Elise –
recalling a name, or a kiss;
the breath our lips shared, unsung song?

When the light has gone, it's music
the dying choose,
if they can, and music we use at their funerals –
the psalms listed in roman numerals;
the soprano singing solo by the grave –
crying, as children do.
Do you think music hath charms?
Do you think music pierces our hearts?

CAROL ANN DUFFY *is Poet Laureate and Professor
of Contemporary Poetry at the Manchester Metropolitan
University.*

Life and Knitting

by SALLY MUIR

❧

Along with life drawing, assembling a flatpack, plumbing and building a fire, every child in every school should be taught to knit. It is an immensely useful skill, and given the uncertain future of our weather, it could prove indispensable as we huddle round our fires in the long hard winters ahead. If you can knit you will be able to make all kinds of useful survival items. With a couple of saplings and some rope you could knit a shelter, as well as the more obvious possibilities of knitted clothing to keep you warm: sweaters, coats, gloves, hats, socks, blankets, etc. With a little ingenuity you could also knit traps, nets, snowshoes and a tent.

Wool is a perfect material, it's organic, renewable, and it embodies all those planet-saving good things that we care about. It is the complete antithesis of artificial fleece, which is made from petrol-chemicals. I very much hope that when our oil supplies dry up, so will the supplies of that work of the devil – the zip-up fleece. Wool, unlike fleece, is a natural insulator, is breathable and doesn't melt if it gets near a naked flame.

One of the joys of knitting, and there are many, is that it is very simple, you hardly need any equipment, just two needles and some sort of yarn. It doesn't even have to be wool; you can knit with anything: hair, string, plastic bags, wire, spaghetti. The basics are very easy and once you learn them you can go as plain or complicated as you like. It's the versatility of knitting that makes it so wonderful, you can knit pretty much anything, from the severely practical to the fabulously useless.

People who knit are, on the wholes relaxed, kind and generous. They are also amazingly inventive. Many of them are Internet users and keen to share information, patterns and advice. Trawling knitting websites can throw up a bizarre selection from the wilder shores of the knitters' imaginations. My recent discoveries have included knitted shields which go over washing machines, kettles and dishwashers 'for people who feel they are sensitive to the electromagnetic fields in their household appliances', a knitted decapitated horsehead, a dissected lab rat, hand grenade, Dalek, an entire digestive system, coral reef, and full-size Ferrari. The late great Oliver Postgate's Clangers were knitted. If you want to find a free pattern to knit your own Clanger, you can. In Bradford-on-Avon, near where I live, a group of knitters have got together and knitted themselves a zebra crossing with cycle-powered Belisha beacon. It's made out of recycled plastic bags, and is now available for hire by other towns with 'similar pedestrian unfriendly concerns'. My business partner Joanna Osborne and I have, in our own small way, contributed to the wealth of improbable patterns with our book of knitted pet accessories, which includes the anti-firework dog balaclava and tortoise hibernation tent.

I have been knitting for about forty-five years, since I was taught at school by Sister Mary Joseph. We were taught knitting so that we could make mittens for the poor babies in Calcutta. It was the sort of thing you did in a convent in the 1960s: it wasn't all Carnaby Street and The Beatles for most of us. I think the nuns were working on the 'devil makes work for idle hands' principle, and in a way they were right. One great advantage of an evening spent knitting is that you can't easily smoke, play video games, buy things from Amazon, or inject drugs at the same time. In fact there are all kinds of things you can't do, as both hands are fully occupied. You can, however, indulge in some bad television, salving your conscience with the thought that you are doing something constructive at the same time.

🖝 SALLY MUIR *is half of Muir and Osborne, the other half being Joanna Osborne. Both have been knitwear designers for many years and are bringing out a new book this year,* Best in Show, Knit Your Own Dog.

In Love with the Clarinet

by GEOFF MULGAN

～

I came late to the idea that blowing makes you happy. But two years ago a friend persuaded me to learn the clarinet, and so whenever I have a free moment I blow. Sometimes I blow hard, sometimes I blow soft, sometimes I blow sweetly and sometimes what comes out is ugly, strained or off-key. But invariably, even if my playing doesn't, sadly, make all of my listeners happy, I feel revived and reconnected to something fundamental by driving air through wood and reed.

I've often wondered why this is, and why something as simple as blowing through a small instrument should have such an effect. I know that we all appear to be born with a music instinct and that from the very earliest times our ancestors fashioned bones and branches into flutes and pipes, perhaps to mimic the birds. But that doesn't quite explain why playing wind instruments feels different in nature from playing instruments with strings or skins.

Part of the explanation may lie in the link between blowing and breathing. To blow you have to become conscious of your breathing and by being conscious of breathing you also become conscious of life. This was the great insight of the yogic teachers: prana, breath, was seen as a life force that had to be restrained and tamed ('yana') on the way to enlightenment.

Another link is that between blowing and flowing. Many of us learned some time ago from the great psychologist Mihaly Csikszentmihalyi that the best way to happiness is to become immersed in activities with flow: activities we lose ourselves in, that stretch our abilities, that help us suspend the anxious sense of self that otherwise intrudes. Blowing is a perfect route to flow, and the very greatest blowers (think of John Coltrane, some of whose performances can now be seen on YouTube) become carried away, their eyes closed, their bodies rising and falling with the torrent of notes.

And blowing, at least where musical instruments are concerned, is also about bending. Having been brought up as a pianist, what I love about the clarinet is that every note can twist and turn, and come alive by being bent. When Immanuel Kant wrote that out of the crooked timbre of humanity no straight thing was ever made, he was thinking about wood, not the tone of musical notes, but he could have been referring to the odd way in which, in music, it's the slight imperfections, the movements off-key and off-colour that are often the most beautiful.

And then finally for true happiness we need, at least sometimes, to blow with others, perhaps in an orchestra or a brass band. William McNeil's remarkable book

Keeping Together in Time suggests that humanity has always been shaped by the experiences of dancing, singing or playing with others. Community truly comes alive through rhythm, through getting lost (again) in movements in sync with others.

Playing music isn't completely free. I had to buy an instrument (albeit second-hand) and reeds don't come for nothing. But blowing into a reed doesn't require any electricity, and there's no risk of feeling guilty about leaving it on standby. You don't have to get dressed, or ask permission. You can take a wind instrument anywhere, and play sitting by a river or on a sand dune, naked or in a dinner jacket, and either way feel strangely free. And if the doctors are to be believed, blowing frequently and furiously enough may even stave off dementia. Who could ask for more?

GEOFF MULGAN *is director of the Young Foundation, which combines research, creating new organisations and enterprises, and local projects across the UK. He has previously been a head of strategy in the government and was founder of the thinktank Demos.*

A Good Log Fire

by ANN WIDDECOMBE

~

There is nothing so good for the soul, the nerves or the overactive mind as the log fire. No long walk on Dartmoor is complete without a collapse in front of the cheerfully crackling logs to round it off.

A roaring fire brings a room alive, more so, of course, if there is a cat purring before it or crumpets gently toasting on long forks or Father Christmas consuming his sherry and mince pies, but even on its own it proclaims the very existence of home. What is the point of reading a book if you cannot look into the flames and meditate between chapters? Or watching some soothing old film without the rustle of burning wood in the background?

Forget coal. Coal is boring. It hisseth not and it crackleth not and it flameth but little. It serves only to keep the fire going but it has no beauty of its own. That is where the makers of the imitation fires err so disastrously, creating a few gas flames round a heap of fake coal. Logs make a fire and without them there is no fire worthy of the name.

It was when I had a fireplace put into my Fulham flat that I knew my first experiment in home ownership really

did involve a home rather than just a property. I had virtually no money but fallen wood is free and I collected twigs
on long walks, sometimes rejoicing in a stout branch. I did
not have a shawl or a basket and I did not meet the big
bad wolf but in every other way it felt like a fairy story.

I was saddened when my next move, onwards and
upwards, meant a flat with no fire but very soon came a
rural constituency complete with cottage and two log fires.
Many a ministerial red box was completed as the flames
danced but then, alas, in 2005 I became fireless, as the
cottage was sold and my London house had no chimney.
I dare say it was good for the planet but it was no good
for me. Retirement and a house in the country beckoned.

I found some views on Dartmoor. There was also a
house but it was horrible and it had no fireplaces. I reasoned
that I could make fireplaces but could not conjure up the
views so I bought it strictly subject to my obtaining plan-
ning permission for two chimneys before I exchanged
contracts.

Permission granted, I moved in, and before I unpacked
I booked the builder. I did not so much put a fireplace in
the library as build a library round a fireplace. In the lounge
the fire crackled as it was decorated and carpeted and I
knew, even amidst the chaos and the dustsheets and the
packing cases, that I had arrived home.

'You can see pictures in the fire,' my gran used to tell
me, and some of my earliest exercises in imagination were
carried out sitting on the rug in front of the hearth. My

mother used to switch off all the lights and shape shadows on the wall with her hands, here a bird tweeting, there a duck sailing.

No return from boarding school was ever complete without finding a fire waiting for me; no recovery from a cold ever successful without sitting before the flames; no teenage hair truly dry unless combed out in its heat; no book enjoyable without the firelight playing on its cover.

Of course fires call for hard work: carting coal and wood, cleaning grates, building, feeding, cleaning again, but if a friend cannot be bothered then it is somehow shocking, disappointing, as if I had caught them pilfering tuck or betraying a secret. At once that person seems soulless. It is surely not possible to find any effort too much for a fire?

How much history has been made before fires as statesmen talk; how many great works as artists ponder? How many marriage proposals have suddenly been made, unplanned, drawn forth by the promise of domesticity offered by the warmth and homeliness of a log fire? How many stray animals have been granted a home because they made straight for the fire and sat looking wistfully into it?

Real fires are not capricious. They do not fuse or run out of meter. Instead they burn steadily, asking only to be lovingly tended, to be the centre of attention, never to feel neglected. Few can resist them. When people enter a room they make straight for the fire, respectfully leaving the most worn armchair beside it empty as this is certain to be the preserve of the owner, or possibly of the owner's pets.

'I sit beside my lonely fire,' wrote the poet. Rot! He who has a fire is never lonely for he has a warm, soothing, gently murmuring companion for life.

∾ THE RIGHT HONOURABLE ANN WIDDECOMBE *was the MP for Maidstone for twenty-three years. She is the author of four novels and presents television documentaries. She lives on Dartmoor in peace and quiet.*

The Aspiring Pianist

by JOHN JULIUS NORWICH

～

Where have all the pianos gone? In the pre-television days of my youth, almost every house seemed to have one; today pianos are comparative rarities, while those that are kept in tune and whose keys don't stick are rarer still. iPods and their like are, by contrast, everywhere. What nobody appears to understand is how much more fun it is to make your own music than to listen to somebody else doing it.

I gave my first public recital at Wigmore Hall when I was six. My piano teacher (Mrs Dora Milner, the only really good one I ever had) used to hire the Hall for one afternoon a year, and all her pupils – even those, like me, who had only just started – were obliged to perform to an audience consisting exclusively of parents. The piece I played was called *The Snowman*. It allowed regrettably little scope for sensitive interpretation, requiring only one note at a time from each hand, the left precisely copying the right but an octave lower.

I used to play the classics – or tried to – but now I've given them up, for two reasons. The first is that I'm just not good enough to do them justice: if I want to hear

Mozart, I want to hear him properly played, not massacred. The second is that, work at it as I may – and I have worked, very hard indeed – I remain a hopeless sight-reader. Sight-reading is, I have long since concluded, a special, separate gift. Those who do it best have done it since childhood and simply do not see the difficulty; I still panic when faced with the simplest of duets.

On the other hand, I have quite a good musical ear. When on my seventh birthday my mother gave me a ukulele, I quickly mastered the three-chord trick – tonic, dominant seventh, sub dominant – which provides the key to literally thousands of simple tunes. At about fifteen I graduated to the guitar and learned another twenty-odd chords; and when, at about sixty, I decided to concentrate exclusively on the piano (which I had never really deserted), the understanding of harmony that I already had made the crossover easy enough. In consequence, my repertoire is now essentially what can best be described as nightclub: Gershwin, Noël Coward, Cole Porter and the like. I massacre them, too, but somehow don't feel so bad about it.

To anyone considering taking up – or going back to – the piano, I have two pieces of advice. The first is to have a decent instrument. This needn't be expensive: second- or third-hand pianos are available quite cheaply at the regular piano auctions. If space is a consideration, however, please think twice before buying an upright. I loathe uprights; it's sad and, I feel, antisocial to play facing the wall. Far better to get a small electronic job. Nowadays these sound like pianos, feel like pianos, operate like pianos. You can look over the top of them into the room, and they never go out of tune. And – unless you really want vibraphone obbligatos or bossa nova rhythms – go for the cheapest and simplest.

My second piece of advice is to take immense care over your choice of teacher. With a good teacher one longs for the next lesson; a bad teacher can reduce the whole thing to drudgery. But remember too that teachers are at best only guides; your real teacher is yourself, when you practise. And that is something you absolutely must be prepared to do: to practise regularly, every day. If you don't, you'll never get any better and will quickly become discouraged. Besides, you'll be throwing money away. If you practise, you'll be astonished at how rapidly you will improve.

But perhaps you know the basics already and don't need a teacher at all – or have anyway decided to do without one. In that case, beg, borrow or steal – you might even buy – a little book called *Playing the Piano for Pleasure* by an American called Charles Cooke. (It is long out of print, but you can probably find a copy through Amazon.) Cooke was a brilliant but hardworking journalist on the *New Yorker* who loved the piano and devoted exactly one hour to it every day of his life. His book – a little gem which deserves republishing – tells us what he played, how he divided his practice time (exercises, sight-reading and working on the pieces themselves), what problems he encountered and how he dealt with them. It is written with the lightest of touches, and every sentence radiates the sheer joy that his piano gives him.

I, alas, have not the discipline of Mr Cooke. But I have no doubt at all that I share his joy – every bit of it. To this day I find it difficult to see a piano without longing to play it, and that joy wells up inside me as soon as I sit down and look at the keyboard. It's a pity, in a way, that I'm such a rotten pianist – but then all great pianists are professionals, with a job to do. I, like Mr Cooke, play for pleasure; and that is surely the greatest reward of all.

~ JOHN JULIUS NORWICH *is the author of histories of Venice, Byzantium, Norman Sicily and the Mediterranean. He has done week-long seasons at the Jermyn Street and Gate Theatres, reading from his anthologies and singing songs to the piano.*

On Cleaning
by MARY KILLEN

～

'It's never as bad as your own,' goes the cliché with regard to washing up. I disagree. I know for a fact that it's never as good as my own. I rarely get the chance to do my own washing up but when I do – usually early on a Sunday morning with Radio 4's *On Your Farm* and *Sunday* for company – it is just at the time when the sun is shafting into my tiny little kitchen. I know I will experience the simple satisfaction of seeing a visible transformation from bad to good, and all of it executed by my own hand.

I don't have the chance to clean very often. Earning the money to keep the cottage over my head comes first in the pecking order of time parcel distribution. I earn money by writing. Writing work is very time-consuming because what's easy to read is hard to write.

By contrast, with cleaning and tidying you can walk into a room where chaos reigns, and slowly but surely re-introduce order. More is the new less and these days we all have too much stuff: too many clothes, too many books, too much mail, too much make-up. But on those days when you have the rare pocket of time to tackle it, you can go forth and wreak the opposite of havoc.

I enjoy ironing for the heat and the instant result as well as for the obvious metaphor. The pile of things needing to be ironed is changed from crumpled to smooth. You can make a miniature stack worthy of an Irish Linen store. It is so enjoyable that I have to stagger it and only allow myself one piece of ironing for every five pieces of grot filing.

I iron in my bedroom because there is a good view from there. I pick up ten pieces of grot discarded in my bedroom by my daughters and transport them to their own bedrooms. I then give myself the thrill of ironing something like a white double sheet, and so it goes on.

Cleaning the windows is another thrill. I was around when the builders put the windows in and I made sure they would be cleanable from the inside as well as the outside so both halves open outwards. It makes all the difference.

Then dust removal. I collect spiders on the end of a long stick duster and release them out of the window. I pull hairs out of hairbrushes and put the hair out of the window too because our sparrows like making nests with it.

The most enjoyable cleaning of all is when I have a friend to stay named Anne who knows how to sew from the days when convent schoolgirls were compulsorily obliged to learn dressmaking. Who on earth had the bright idea of stopping that? Anne sits mending complicated rips in my bedlinen while I proceed through the room restoring order and meanwhile downloading the contents of my brain and using her as a psychotherapist.

Why has cleaning been downgraded to the status of drudgery? If I were to say that cleaning was my hobby people would think I was mad. Yet simple mechanical tasks of the sort that make a huge and visible difference are the most gratifying pursuits of all.

◆ MARY KILLEN *is a regular contributor to the* Spectator.

PART THREE

Creature Comforts

Grooming the Dog

by ROY HATTERSLEY

❧

It was a nightly ritual for fifteen years and, after a break of three months, it has become a nightly ritual again. Thank heavens for that. Without the joy of putting a dog to bed, I did not sleep so well myself. Do not mistake my need to end each day this way as intellectually perverse. Not one item in the essential procedure can be attributed to acceptance of the anthropomorphic fallacy. I have never thought of dogs as human. But from time to time I do think of myself as a dog. In that persona, I have no doubt that ten minutes' care and attention before the lights are switched off is a canine necessity. In my *Homo sapiens* mode, I welcome it as another opportunity to express and experience what makes the world go round. That is what dogs are for.

Although the last walk of the day is an essential preliminary, it is only on rainy nights that it makes a contribution to the ritual. Drying a wet dog is, in itself, one of life's joys, for it gratifies several senses at once. An enterprising cosmetic company ought to bottle and market a smell which is, metaphorically at least, essence of dog. The fragrance accompanies the tactile joy of rubbing the dog dry – making sure not to miss the concealed places at which, I was taught as a boy, a dog is most vulnerable. It is important to begin the drying process as soon as the rain-soaked walk ends – not because quick action makes the difference between robust health and pneumonia but because, given the chance to shake, a wet dog can destroy a whole room.

It goes without saying that the brushing – like stroking – must be with, rather than against, the direction in which the fur lies. But it is also necessary to avoid sensitive parts and places. Indeed if a wire brush is being used, it is essential. In my experience, dogs – which by their nature enjoy having their backs scratched – welcome a brisk metallic scrape along the spine. But Buster, at least, was not keen on the same treatment being applied to his genitals – even though he had no genitals to speak of. With Jake, the much lamented successor of Buster, care has to be taken at both ends – even with the bristle, that is to say plastic, brush. Jake is an English bull terrier, which means that his extended snout has virtually no hair at all. I regard him as colour coded. The brushing rule is 'Avoid all the pink bits.'

Jake is only just beginning to cooperate in the high-point of the nightly ritual – cleaning the teeth. Buster accepted the idea because the invitation to advertise 'Pet Smiles Week' contributed to the publicity for his first book. I cooperated after I saw the video which illustrated the horrific consequences of leaving a dog's teeth to rot. After a week or two, Buster refused to go to bed until the job was done – not because of his enthusiasm for dental hygiene but because he had become addicted to the toothpaste which smelled of rotting game. We are persisting in preserving Jake's molars even though cleaning his teeth raises new areas to work on with his training regime.

The best teeth-cleaning posture is what in heraldry is called 'rampant' – that is the position of the dog not the human. The human sits on a hard chair, an image which is rarely included in coats of arms. Rampant posture requires the dog to stand on its hind legs with its front paws on the human's knees. But for most of the day we try to stop Jake doing just that. According to experts in canine psychology, a dog – allowed to lean on its owner – develops the belief that he or she is the dominant partner in the relationship – something I never minded when Buster was on the other end of the toothbrush, because he was the undisputed leader of the pack. As he grew old, he gradually sank down from balancing on two legs to standing on four, then to sitting and finally to what the Royal College of Heralds calls 'couchon'. I expected that Jake, not yet a year old, would approach teeth cleaning in dominant mode. In stead he lies on his back and kicks his legs in the air – changing the problem from the psychological undesirability of allowing him to believe that he is boss to the more practical difficulty of getting the brush in his mouth.

I shall persevere. Proper care, during the last half-hour

of the day, is essential to a dog's welfare. What is more, I love it. Preparing for bed is one of life's great pleasures.

✒ ROY HATTERSLEY *is a politician turned writer and journalist. He was a member of Harold Wilson's Government and Jim Callaghan's Cabinet and Deputy Leader of the Labour Party. He has published twenty-four books, his most recent being a biography of Lloyd George.*

In Pursuit of the Purple Emperor
by MATTHEW OATES

~

Like the sukebind in Stella Gibbons' *Cold Comfort Farm*, the Purple Emperor butterfly generates bizarre human behaviour and is highly addictive. It is also our national butterfly, only being British we have yet to recognise it as such.

For one heady month in midsummer the Emperor takes to the air, and people vulnerable to obsessive behaviour go quite silly. Woodland car parks overflow with vehicles belonging to butterfly enthusiasts, thrill-seekers and curious minds, all after a glimpse of an insect that is elusive, scarce and utterly unpredictable, and which lives largely in the tree tops. A typical sighting consists of a dark object the size of a small bat hurtling over the crown of an oak tree, often in pursuit of some petrified small bird. Was it a vision or a waking dream? It is both, and more.

The dog-walkers suffer most. For eleven months of the year the woods are theirs, then the sukebind blooms and chaos ensues. Bizarre humanoids bedecked with cameras and binoculars patrol the woodland rides, one eye ceaselessly scanning the oak tops, the other seeking an Emperor breakfasting on canine or fox deposits. This butterfly does not visit dainty flowers, but seeks minerals from revolting excrescences along woodland paths. Victorian butterfly collectors ruthlessly exploited this habit, staking out dead rabbits and worse. Think Emperor, think Rome; think Caligula, Commodus and Nero: think worse, and you are approaching the Purple Emperor's level of depravity.

Recently, a Japanese butterfly expert discovered that Purple Emperors love oriental shrimp paste. So do dogs. They eat it, roll in it, and regurgitate it in their owner's cars. So today's butterfly enthusiasts – benign photographers in the main – liberally bedeck the woodland rides with smelly offerings. Yes, the dog-walkers truly suffer.

One does not forget one's first Emperor (5.15 p.m., 5 July 1970, Dragons Green, West Sussex: imprint, absolute). Nor does one forget the Emperor's afternoon aerial displays around his 'Master Trees', the sacred groves where males gather annually for courtship and mating and testosterone-fuelled combat while waiting for the giant Empress to appear in need of their services. Here, male belligerence knows no bounds. Anything that invades male airspace is intercepted and pursued, be it butterfly, bird (large or small) or high-flying aircraft.

When two Emperors meet, utter hatred breaks out. To anthropomorphise further, think Liverpool vs Manchester United, add England vs Australia, and keep going; eventually you will reach the level of rivalry of male Emperors. When two meet in mid-air, their language is purple, which is worse than blue. They circle each other in ire, before one chases the other off, out of sight and mind, at great speed. The victorious gladiator returns. Think Emperor, think Rome; think violence, and admire.

The point of these purple passages is that Miss Gibbons was correct in that we need an official Silly Season. But with the Emperor, silliness is juxtaposed with the beauty and wonder of nature that reaches far into the inner soul. If you have yet to encounter the Purple Emperor then do so. Visit his website, www.thepurpleempire.com, and himself. Take a deckchair, a large jug of Pimm's, the newspaper, *Test Match Special*, and enjoy. But leave the dog behind.

One morning at the zenith of last June, I blundered into a new dimension. I had been probing its boundaries for some time, unwittingly; then, without warning, crossed over, for the passion had deemed itself ripe. Yes, once in a purple moon the Emperor changes his colours. Known as aberration Iole, after a princess whose desirability led to the death of Heracles, this excessively rare colour form lacks the white bands and spots. Iole is the ultimate quarry of every butterfly enthusiast.

Suddenly – and I had warned you about visions and waking dreams – there it was, the subject of my wildest aspirations, a pristine Iole male imbibing some mysterious ambrosia on the woodland floor. The experience realised one of those dreams that means all and everything to the dreamer without meaning anything to anyone else. Such desiderata are of the utmost importance, being the passion of the individual soul.

MATTHEW OATES is the Purple Emperor's high servant and one of the country's leading naturalists. His passion for nature's beauty and wonder is total. He works for the National Trust.

Porcine Pleasures
by ROSIE BOYCOTT

～

How could you ever be unhappy in the company of pigs? There they were, six of them, standing in a row on the far side of the fence. They were Gloucester sows and they looked like a group of fat aunts out for a day at the seaside, wearing lopsided polka-dot swimming suits. Their attention was captured by an unruly young boar, a black Berkshire, the breed made famous by P. G. Wodehouse, who created The Empress of Blandings, the Earl of Emsworth's famous sow whose sole interest was eating.

Our pigs liked to eat but they also liked to keep an eye on what was happening around the farm, and right now Earl was emitting wild cries, his four feet rooted firmly in the mud, refusing to budge despite my entire weight pushing on his rear end.

I pulled off my scarf, which happened to be pink – and cashmere – and slung it around his neck and started pulling from the other end, a bitter windfall apple in my hand as a bribe to get him to his field. He shot forward, I fell backwards and the scarf twisted round his neck.

He stood upright, tail spinning round in glee, apple in

mouth, and gazed triumphantly at the Gloucesters. Then he trotted down the lane towards his run, every bit the pig about town, the pink scarf setting off his dense black coat to a tee. Charles Dickens once spied a pig trotting down Broadway in New York. He was entranced by the pig's sense of purpose.

> He leads a roving, gentlemanly, vagabond kind of life, somewhat answering to that of our club men back home. A free and easy, careless, indifferent kind of pig, having a very large acquaintance among pigs of the same character. In this respect a republican pig, going where he pleases and mingling with the best society.

As Earl went through his gate, the scarf caught on the gate post. He looked round in annoyance, bit it neatly in two, and headed for his trough. A free and easy pig indeed.

⬿ ROSIE BOYCOTT *was the founder of* Spare Rib, *and editor of the* Independent, Independent on Sunday *and* Daily Express. *She is the founder of a community farm in Somerset and is currently the Mayor of London's Food Adviser.*

Lambing at Wimpole

by SARAH MUKHERJEE

I went to Wimpole Hall today.

The elegant eighteenth-century Cambridgeshire house itself was closed, its windows shuttered and curtains tied. The path to the farm we have visited so often was secured by a heavy wooden door. But the parkland was walkable. The sun, set in a sky of palest blue, was barely warmer than a whisper, and the grey-green trees, silhouettes lichen-softened, stood stolidly in the mud created by weeks of melted snow and rain.

The heavy snow that took the UK by surprise in recent winters caused inconvenience to millions and brought tragedy to some – but it also restored our sense of seasonality. We had years of grey temperance, where cool and wet melded into warmish and wet and then back again, the only metronomes of our passing years the Christmas lights in the shops and the kids' summer holidays. The snow shocked us back into the sensibilities of our parents and grandparents. Seventy-hour working weeks and twenty-four-hour lifestyles gave way to wondering when it would be safe enough to walk to the bottom of the hill. We got the point of all those things considered too old-fashioned even for 'granny-chic': thermals, hats with ear flaps and local shops.

Of course, it's easy to be nostalgic if you have the twenty-first-century luxury of central heating and the Internet; past and present, those with least suffer most. But the point of those countrywide spring festivals, celebrations created and moulded by centuries of religion and tradition, now become clear. The eggs and the bunnies. New life and full bellies.

Which brings me back to Wimpole Hall farm. In a country where some children think eggs come from sheep, carrots grow on trees and milk is made of flour and water, we as parents are all too aware of the rare opportunities little ones have to see food production up close. Which is presumably why so many of us who live near Wimpole take our kids to see the lambing, an event that combines the wonder of new life with the chaos of an airport lounge during a luggage handlers' strike.

Lambing brings you to the casino of the natural world. Perhaps you will wait for hours by the pens and not see a birth. But you could just as easily arrive to see three pop out, steaming and slimy and (for the mothers among us) fast enough to induce some jealousy.

Something as commonplace, in the wider scheme of things, as the birth of a lamb becomes a special event. There is a hush of anticipation as the shepherds mark out the next ewe that's likely to give birth. They pen her up.

Whispered updates on the labour susurrate through the crowd.

Silence. A tiny cry. And the sudden exhalation of a hundred people, realising they have been holding their breath in anticipation of that first, thin wail of life.

~ SARAH MUKHERJEE *is the BBC's environment correspondent.*

Walking the Dog
by TREVOR GROVE

If there is one thing more pleasureable than going for a walk, it is going for a walk with a dog. Strolling, rambling, hiking and even jogging are all very well. But not as well as they could be with the addition of a canine companion. What I say is, given a choice of walking partner, two legs good, four legs better.

Dog-lovers do not need persuading of this. If a dog's chief attraction for its owner is unconditional loyalty, owners generally reciprocate, however ugly, fat and disobedient the mutt in question. In this country, such devotion is marked by at least one walk a day, if only for hygiene purposes. Elsewhere in the world there is no such moral imperative. Dogs are kept on chains, in yards or in escape-proof gardens. If they get a walk at all in, say, Rome or Buenos Aires, it is only as part of a dozen-strong pack held in check by an out-of-work actor with a cigarette in his mouth, leaning back on his fistful of leads like a charioteer. Here in Britain, however, we are grateful to our dogs for making us feel virtuous, forcing us to take exercise and propelling us out of doors whatever the weather. Walking the dog is thus a rich source of smugness, a pleasure that's not available to the owners of other pets, such as cats and gerbils, or no pets at all.

There are, though, loftier reasons for recommending the dog as a walking companion. The thing about a dog is that he or she is a sort of go-between, linking Man, with whom dogs mainly live, and the Wild, whose call still howls in their doggy ears. After millennia of evolution, the genetic differences between *Canis familiaris* and *Canis lupus* are undetectable. You only have to look into a Husky's wolfish eyes to know how Mowgli felt. And even a Yorkie with a red bow on his head has, in his tiny way, the characteristic instincts of his grim, grey ancestor. Despite the startling difference in size and appearance, they each recognise the dog beneath the skin, the wolf within.

So when you walk with a dog, it's to be accompanied by a being far more in touch with the natural world than you or even David Attenborough. On a country walk it will be the dog that lets you know of the grouse in the heather, the shrew in the long grass, and raises its nose to the rank whiff of *Vulpes vulpes*.

On Hampstead Heath, where I do most of my dog-walking, there are plenty of foxes and small mousy creatures scuttling through the undergrowth, but no grouse. What there are, though, are masses of squirrels. Strictly speaking, letting dogs chase them must be against the hunting ban. But I've only once seen one caught and it immediately wriggled free – which is just as well or we'd have the Hampstead branch of the League Against Cruel Sports sabotaging our morning meets.

My Dalmatian, Jasper, was an enthusiastic squirrel-hunter in his youth. But after hundreds of fruitless pursuits which ended up with him splatting into a tree-trunk like a cartoon character, he learned wisdom. Nowadays, at the great age of seven, Jasper will only give chase if the quarry is out in the open, well away from aerial escape routes. It is a sign of his canine cunning that whenever he does spot a foolish young squirrel in such circumstances, he no longer aims at the prey itself but races directly towards the nearest tree, knowing this is where it will make for, which it always does – an impressive case of self-taught triangulation. But still, no dice. Just as Jasper's about to cut it off at the pass, the artful dodger jinks, leaps, and hits the bark just ahead of the bite, before scampering aloft.

But maybe the best thing about walking a dog is to enjoy its encounters with other dogs. There is no better lesson in multicultural, non-racist, un-sizeist, non-sexist, live-and-let-live friendliness than the way one dog meets another in a public space. Territorial defensiveness may change the picture in the home or farmyard. But where two or more dogs gather in the open, the understanding between them (after a quick smell-check), is almost always polite. Irish terrier and English setter, Border collie and German shepherd, Pekinese and Pomeranian, dogs of every breed and none greet, sniff, wag their tails more or less vigorously and pass on with perfect social poise.

The novelist Elizabeth von Arnim called her wonderfully original autobiography, first published in 1936, *All The Dogs Of My Life*. It opens with the unforgettable line: 'I would like, to begin with, to say that though parents, husbands, children, lovers, and friends are all very well, they are not dogs.' Quite so.

TREVOR GROVE *is the author of* One Dog and His Man: Notes from an All-Weather Walker.

Collecting the Eggs

by JONATHAN DIMBLEBY

Every morning when I am at home, regardless of the weather, I go out of the back door in my dressing gown and wellingtons. My dog, Sam, comes with me. We walk across the lawn under the beech tree and into the orchard. If it is bright the birds are singing and a swarm of them are feeding at one or other of the (relatively) squirrel-proof feeders. They fly away momentarily as we pass but are soon back to guzzle again. I walk through the longer grass – sometimes mushy after rain, sometimes snow-covered, often frosty – and the hens hear me and start to murmur. I open the shed door and the three of them – Truffle, Amber and Pearl – walk in stately procession into the light of day.

They peck neatly at the grass for a few moments. And then, as if with a sudden memory of yesterday's good things, one of them lifts her head and sets off at speed, wings flapping, towards the feeders to pick at the discarded grain on the ground below. The other two race to catch up. I steal a hand into the nesting box and usually find one or two and sometimes three eggs, not yet quite cold. It is an exquisite moment.

I walk back to the house glancing up at my wind turbine. If the atmospheric pressure is high and the air is crisp but still, the turbine is immobile, mocking my heavy investment in renewable energy. But it doesn't matter; it is a sweet morning and a fine, misty view across the fields towards the sea. If the wind is blowing and the rain is in stair-rods, it doesn't matter either; the turbine is whirring away and I am saving the planet.

I go back inside and show the morning's catch to my wife and the little ones. I then pencil the date on them and place them in bowl on the sideboard and sit down for family breakfast and my porridge. Could there be any better start to the day?

JONATHAN DIMBLEBY is a writer and broadcaster, who has has presented Radio 4's Any Questions? *for over twenty years. His most recent BBC2 series* Africa – A Journey with Jonathan Dimbleby *was transmitted in June 2010. He is a former president of the Soil Association and the Campaign to Protect Rural England.*

In Praise of Zoos

by ALAIN DE BOTTON

People look at you strangely if you make a trip to the zoo without a child. You should ideally have a gang of children, evidence of dribbled ice cream and some balloons as well. Contemplating zoo enclosures with oriental small-clawed otters or leopard geckos hardly seems an adult way to pass the afternoon. The elegant question in London at present is whether you've caught the Ingres show at the National Gallery, not the new pygmy hypo at Regent's Park zoo.

But my five-year-old nephew pulled out at the last minute (he'd remembered it was his best friend's birthday), and I stubbornly decided to go through with our afternoon as planned. My first thought – after buying an ice cream, though not a balloon – was how strange animals look. Apart from the odd cat, dog or horse, it's years since I've seen a real animal, an extraordinary, jungle-bookish sort of creature. Take the camel: a U-shaped neck, two furry pyramids, eyelashes that seem coated in mascara, and a set of yellow buck teeth. There was a guide on hand with some facts: camels can go ten days in the desert without drinking; their humps aren't filled with water, it's fat; the eyelashes are designed to keep out sandstorms; and their liver and kidneys extract all moisture from food, leaving their dung dry and compact. They're some of the best adapted creatures on the planet, concluded the guide – at which point I experienced a childish burst of jealousy at the inadequacy of the human liver and kidney, and our lack of furry bumps to cut out the need for a mid-afternoon snack.

If creatures end up looking so strange, it's a sign of their adaptation to the natural environment, said Darwin, and no one would doubt it in Regent's Park. The Sri Lankan sloth bear has long mobile lips and two missing upper incisors so that it can suck ants and termites out of their nests, a distinctive facial feature which no one who relied on lunch from a deli would bother with. I had some melancholy thoughts finishing my ice cream staring at some tar-coloured, pygmy hippos wallowing in mud. The word dinosaur came to mind, not that they resembled them, but they evoked the dinosaur as a byword for fatally slow adaptation to an environment. There are only a few of them left in the world; the future in their natural African habitats lies with lither, more libidinous gazelle-like things.

A zoo visit proves the cliché that it takes all sorts. Every creature seems wonderfully adapted for some things, hopelessly suited for others. The horseshoe crab could never get in the pages of *Vogue* (it looks like a miniature military helmet with bow legs), and couldn't read Gibbon, but it's a star at surviving in deep water and not getting eaten by sharks. It lives quietly, sliding occasionally across the ocean floor to grab a mollusc.

It's hard not to identify with animals, not to land on creatures one might name if forced into an after-dinner round of what-would-you-be-if-you-had-to-be-an-animal game (sadly losing out to Pictionary as evening entertainment). Flaubert loved the game; in his letters, he compared himself variously to a boa constrictor (1841), an oyster in its shell (1845), and a hedgehog rolling up to protect itself (1853, 1857). I came away identifying with the Malayan tapir, the baby okapi, the llama and the turtle (especially on Sunday evenings).

A zoo unsettles in simultaneously making animals seem more human and humans more animal. 'Apes are man's closest relative,' reads a caption by the orang-utan enclosure. 'How many similarities can you see?' Far too many for comfort, of course. Shave him, dress him in a T-shirt and tracksuit bottoms, and the one scratching his nose in the corner of the cage is a cousin of mine, except that Joe has a large flat in Belsize Park and spent two weeks in Dorset with his kids this summer. In May 1842, Queen Victoria visited Regent's Park zoo, and in her diary, noted of a new orang-utan from Calcutta: 'He is wonderful, preparing and drinking his tea, but he is painfully and disagreeably human.' (Reading this, I imagine being captured and placed in a cage like a room in a Holiday Inn, with three meals a day passed through a hatch, and nothing to do other than watch TV – while a crowd of giraffes look on at me, giggling and videoing, licking giant ice creams, while saying what a short neck I have.)

Inevitably perhaps, I walk out of the zoo with a pair of Desmond Morris spectacles. Calling Sarah up for dinner loses its innocence; it's merely part of the mating ritual of the human species, not fundamentally different from what llamas are up to when they start to whistle strangely at each other on autumn nights.

Then again, there is relief to be found in the ability to view one's antics as complex manifestations of essentially simple animal drives; for food, shelter and survival of one's genetic offspring. I may take out a yearly membership for Regent's Park zoo.

↝ ALAIN DE BOTTON *is an author of nine non-fiction books and the founder of two organisations, Living Architecture and The School of Life, the former dedicated to promoting beauty, the latter wisdom.*

Owls at Night

by ANTONY BEEVOR

I always feel a frisson of strange joy at night when, awake in bed, I suddenly hear the eerie, wavering call of tawny owls in our wood. As a metaphor for ghostliness and mystery, the owl has long played a symbolic role in English poetry, to say nothing of our gothic novels. It is an integral part of our folklore as a bird of ill omen. Fortunately, the owl is no longer a figment of evil in the rustic imagination, but although no longer persecuted, its numbers have still not recovered. We are privileged to have three species in our small wood: barn owls (whose ghostly presence we so rarely see), tawny owls and little owls, who perch out on our fence-posts. In the mating season we occasionally hear owls during the day calling in the wood, and sometimes an answer comes from another wood across the valley. But nothing gives me such a shiver of pleasure as the long, quavering hoot at night.

ANTONY BEEVOR *is the author of* Stalingrad, Berlin: The Downfall 1945, The Battle for Spain *and* D-Day: the Battle for Normandy. *He lives in deepest Kent.*

PART FOUR

The Great Outdoors

Running in the Rain

by PATRICK BARKHAM

～

The world has woken up grey and cold and damp: the kind
of weather that makes your joints creak and complain even
when you are perfectly well. Half asleep, I pull on some
shorts and stumble onto the dark ribbon of wet road. At
first, it does not feel as bad as I feared. And then I turn a
corner and pellets of rain smack me about the chops.

My thighs are as cold as gravestones. My knuckles are
swinging balls of lead. The chill sets my face into a crimson
grimace. I catch sight of it in the window of the dry-
cleaner's on the corner. Pad, pad, pad, go my trainers, first
on the pavement and then with a thud and a splash, I
swerve onto the old railway line. This muddy embankment
curves through the Victorian suburbs of north London, a
hidden treat that even in winter can fool you into thinking
you are alone in the countryside.

Why go outside when the weather is so horrible? And
if you must go out, why not walk, like one or two other
hardy souls cocooned in coats as big as duvets, their heads
down like billy goats about to butt?

As children, if we were unloaded into a lovely landscape,

a beach or a wood, we would run. The countryside calls for it. Poor are those people who are capable of trotting five yards yet only ever walk across wet sand and never hurdle a puddle with a heart-skip of elation.

There is a nothingness to a raw winter's day. The cold does not smell of anything. The skies are almost empty, except for a solitary seagull. Everyone is indoors. All is silent apart from the bitter wind that moans in my ears like a whale. It brings a glorious sense of solitude. I feel like the only runner in Britain. As Alan Sillitoe's untamed young offender put it: 'It's a treat being a long-distance runner, out in the world by yourself with not a soul to make you bad-tempered or tell you what to do.'

My legs warm up. They have become the colour of a side of raw beef expertly handled in the butcher's. The deserted track slowly rises towards Highgate and a robin finds its voice under a dripping dark bush. A blackbird as well, hopping further into the undergrowth as I sweat-splash past. A crunched can of 1664 and a fading Pot Noodle tub are exposed beneath the skeletons of last year's hogweed.

Wherever I am, I run in the rain. When I lived in Sydney I would seek out stormy days and run when cool rain blew in and the light dimmed to levels that reminded me of England. When I go home to Norfolk, I run through its more cautious rain, past a field of liquid mud where pigs raise their heads and study me shrewdly. On days like these, another living thing is an event. In the tunnel of trees on the old railway line I pass an old man and a retriever the colour of summer sand, except for its booties made of mud.

It is a cliché that running can sort out your head. You may feel calmer but nothing really gets settled. When the going is good, I think about all the things that I have done and all the things I should do; reparations I should make to loved ones and idle fantasies about speeches I will never give and emails I will never send. A cacophony of chatter like the skein of geese arrowing overhead. Fatigue comes and goes as randomly as a gust of wind. But when it arrives, it chases all other thoughts away. Moving my limbs feels a self-conscious act again and I focus on coaxing them along, or check up on aches and pains as they pop up in different places.

At the top of the hill, where the former railway finally gives up against the incline and sinks into a tunnel, I pause, breathless, and look down on Archway Bridge. The city below has been wiped out by the rain. The citadels of capitalism, the whole screeching madness of our global financial system, do not exist at that moment. The only sign of life comes from the distant groan of a tower crane a mile beyond.

Turning for home, my footsteps fall heavier. Back on the streets, the noise of the heavy tyres of a bus is deafening. A number 29 throws a brown curtain of gritty water over my shins. Almost unseeing now, I cross the road when the traffic parts as miraculously as a biblical sea.

Arriving home is a delicious ritual: the glass of cold water, down in one slug; unpeeling running gear in the warmth; entering a golden hour, floating on a high, in which anything seems possible. The only thing left to run? A bath.

PATRICK BARKHAM *is a features writer for the* Guardian *and author of* The Butterfly Isles – A Summer in Search of Our Emperors and Admirals.

Looking Up

by LUCINDA LAMBTON

❧

'To look up is to learn to love architecture' is my daily, hourly and by-the-minute mantra. It never lets me down. How else can you drink in ever-flowing draughts of shock and surprise; of excitement, discovery and delight? Look around and about you, and best of all above you, and, more often than not, you will see something that will straightway suffuse you with satisfaction. Such pleasures as spotting these buildings are simple, hugely important and as free as the air in which they stand.

Take a leaf out of my book: when boarding an aeroplane at Heathrow, look up and spot the spire of Stanwell's church. 'To be in Heathrow is to be in the historic bosom of the British Isles,' wrote a Mr J. Pendral Brodhurst in the 1930s when Hounslow Heath was still asleep; 'with its pure sweet air of antiquity in interest it is unapproachable in the land.' Today, one look at the soaring presence of the thirteenth-, fourteenth- and fifteenth-century St Mary's – only feet from Runway 5 – and you can still breathe, through the jet fumes, that 'pure sweet air of antiquity'. Furthermore, Lord Knyvett, who foiled the Gunpowder

Plot, lies in the chancel, beneath his larger than life-size marble effigy, a monument writhed about with primrose-wreathed skulls of translucent alabaster. All rare ruminations to be enjoyed – and there are many many more hereabouts – thanks to having looked up and seen the spire of St Mary's Church.

The same goes for the corner of West High Street and Fawcett Street in Sunderland. Gloomily plodding rather than walking, in the pouring rain, muttering my mantra 'Look up . . .', I obeyed. Shutting my eyes past the annihilating-your-sensibilities blue RBS fascia, then *Abracadabra!* there were three faience elephants waving their trunks on high. Each of them standing beneath a barge-boarded Gothic canopy, they are all surrounded by what can only be described as a frenzy of Hindu and Gothic decoration. With brilliant polychrome brickwork, terracotta and faiencework by Doulton, ornate stone carvings, innovative use of concrete, crockets, finials and gargoyles galore, architectural extravagance here has known no bounds. Alongside bulbously ornamental chimneys, there are also towers and spires and even a minaret. Why did all the elephants have packs on their backs? Because, I was told, this was once the Elephant Tea Rooms, built by Frank Caws for a local tea merchant in 1873 and here were the elephants bearing him the tea. Today, at street level – beneath the wrecking-the-look-of-all-high-streets fascia – banking posters scream their false promises through the windows, giving no hints of the exotic Eastern promises on high. I grew up near

Sunderland; I must have walked past the building many hundreds of times, but never before had I looked up.

Even the daily-tramped-along-by-millions Old and New Bond Streets, bang in the middle of London, never fail to surprise. At first the ever-evolving designer glitz of their shops at street level actually blind you to seeing that there is any building above them at all. Look up and there is an architectural feast, dating from the early eighteenth to the twentieth century, and of every conceivable style. From the quietly classical to the ragingly ornate Renaissance; from bulging nudes to art deco detailing. There are abstract panels by Henry Moore, as well as a sculpture of steel by Maurice Lambert. A Gothic gable of 1926 spikes into the sky, and then there are naked caryatids of 1906 on parade in an Ionic colonnade. Maybe a good deal is neo-this and neo-that but there it all is nevertheless; yet, I would like to wager, unseen by passers-by. What too about spotting the sculpture of the lion-headed Egyptian god Sekhmet dating from 1320 BC? It hangs in the gabled porch of Sotheby's in New Bond Street. With London's long central spine of Old and New Bond Street, I can rest my case.

Times without number, by a mere lift of the chin and an upward glance, my soul has soared; be it thanks to a Tooting drainpipe head, that looks for all the world like a miniature church pulpit in which a tiny parson might at any moment appear, or otherwise to the sculpted heads of five prime ministers decorating Gothic arches on the facade of a sadly dilapidated pub on the outskirts of Manchester. There they all were: Gladstone, Salisbury, Disraeli, Peel and Russell; all looking down onto a thundering main road, but no one was looking up at them.

If you feel that you have been force-fed with surfeit of buildings – hard cheddar! This is my daily diet and I am a very greedy, indeed glutinous woman!

✎ LUCINDA LAMBTON *is a photographer, writer and broadcaster, with some eighty television programmes to her name. Her books include a best-selling history of the lavatory,* Temples of Convenience, *and recent and forthcoming works on architecture for animals, the architectural legacy of the British in the Caribbean, and Queen Mary's doll's house.*

Four Out of Five for Tennis

by RICHARD LAYARD

～

When it examined mental well-being, a recent government report identified five key ingredients for happiness – the equivalent of the daily fruit and veg for physical health. These five ingredients spell out GREAT – Giving, Relating, Exercising, Attending to the world around, and Teaching yourself something. So the moral is 'Be a GREAT person, and be happy'. We shall make that a theme for the Movement for Happiness to be launched next autumn.

But do I follow the advice myself? You can't easily combine all five at once, although tennis nearly does it. The exercise bit is obvious, even if you play doubles. I play with people better than me, ages ranging from 17 to 76. It works best if 76 is paired with 17.

Attention is crucial. You do not think about anything else for an hour and a half. You are in what the psychologists call 'Flow'. You watch the ball. It is not the same as 'savouring', which is the other form of attention, but it engages your body and soul.

As our group gets older, we take the game more and more seriously. Hilarious things happen during rallies, but when we cross sides and sip our Lucozade, we no longer speak. I suppose we are still hoping to improve, forever. And you do learn – you can be taught and you can teach yourself from your mistakes.

But the game itself is less than half of tennis. The worst part is the preparation – without it you would be amazed at what can happen to your Achilles tendon. At least fifteen minutes' stretching is vital, and one of our group also does an hour's mental preparation. Once stretched, you put on the band-aids – the knee band, the elbow support, the toe plasters. These don't show under the tracksuit and of course you wear a cap to hide the bald patch. To the millions who have given up tennis due to tennis elbow, I would say, 'Please come back. Any good physiotherapist can fix it – if you do the stretches.'

That's the worst part. The best part is the relating. After the game we always have a seminar over a drink. Between us our group covers architecture, music, retail, finance, journalism, academia and sixth form, and we are a sort of mutual support group – the opposite of the social isolates so brilliantly described by Robert Putnam in his book *Bowling Alone*. It is unfortunate that to play indoors in winter in this country you more or less have to belong to a club, and that is where we have our seminar. It's a lovely ending to the day, twice a week.

So there you are – four of the five 'be happy' fruit and veg. And what about giving? Giving is about responsibility and I am responsible for getting everyone there. It is the biggest intellectual challenge I face and can only be done with an elaborate matrix of dates and players.

But when I am at the tennis, I am on holiday, with no responsibility. And how do I go to sleep afterwards? Reliving my shots.

〜 RICHARD LAYARD *is the author of* Happiness: Lessons from a New Science, *published in twenty languages. As an economist, he is an expert on unemployment and inequality and he is also a member of the House of Lords.*

Gone Fishing

by TOM FORT

It has often been claimed that the urge to catch a fish springs from some deeply buried inherited memory of our hunter-gatherer past. Maybe. But is that a defence – to claim that we are acting in tune with the vestiges of club and animal skin and cave-dwelling within us? How can you defend an amusement that involves wishing to pull a hook into the mouth of a creature that has done you no harm and intends none.

Although I do all I can – short of not fishing – to minimise the suffering, I do not pretend that it does not exist. I cannot measure a fish's pain or share its terror; but common sense tells me that they are part of its response. My justification – there is no defence – is that the desire, the passion, are part of me. No society has yet deemed fishing a crime; therefore it is no crime; therefore I will fish as long as I wish to, and I will feel no guilt.

The joy in it is very simple and pure. But it is not easy to pin down exactly where it resides. There is pleasure in the anticipation and the preparation. There is keen pleasure in the peace of the riverbank and in the beauty of the river and its plants and creatures. There is the wonder, which never dims, of drawing a fish to the net, taking in the colours and textures of its body, the perfection of design. I like to see them go, too; to hold them with all the gentleness at my disposal as the gills work, until the tail kicks and in a muscular flash it is gone.

If pressed, I suppose I would say that the moment of moments is the moment just before contact. The sunken fly is intercepted, the dry fly is sucked under in a kiss at the surface, the float vanishes and stays vanished. The heart pounds as you strike. Contact is made.

That is the essence of it, very plain and simple. But the possibilities opened up are enormous. As I write this, I am enclosed on three sides by my books about fishing. I have hundreds: books of theory, books of instruction, books of philosophy, books of adventure and reflection. Some are unfailing sources of delight to me, but many are deadly dull. Each of them (I have done a couple myself) was written by someone convinced that they had something especially, even uniquely valuable to say about this simple business of catching a fish.

Minds many times more powerful than mine have devoted incalculable quantities of high-grade brain effort to investigating the minds, tendencies, diets and habits of fish (which have very small brains). Occasionally one of these minds conjures a flash of light in a dark place, but more often the brilliant solution turns out to be merely one possible answer to a very complicated problem.

There are few firm rules in the domain of our finny friends.

A mistake that too many anglers make is to compartmentalise the sport, and thereby shut themselves off from its amazing richness. My local butcher is a mad-keen carp and pike man, but when I enthuse about nymphing for grayling or stalking wild trout with a dry fly, his expression tells me that he does not believe these refinements are for him. Similarly the salmon angler, when told of the thrill of rolling a lump of luncheon-meat under a trailing willow branch in search of a chub or barbel, is likely to respond as if you had let off a stink bomb in his direction. (Is it a coincidence that the majority of the ignorant and ill-informed fishermen I have encountered in an extended fishing life have been salmon men?)

I am inclined to think that fishermen are born and cannot be made, and it follows that the seed is generally sown early. Having flowered and fruited it can become dormant – one of my dearest fishing friends gave it up for years, then came back to it with passion renewed – but if well rooted it will last a lifetime. My rugby days are long behind me, and although I still play cricket, I acknowledge that I am a creaking, rheumatic shadow of the fine figure in flannels I once cut. But the fishing goes on, and I have every hope that – assuming the legs and arms and spirit are willing – it will last into the winter of my days. And I trust that when I can no longer wade or see a hatching olive or flex my fly rod, there will be someone to take me beside the stream, to watch – or even just to listen to – the water, which is where the mystery and the joy are found.

TOM FORT *is a journalist and writer. He worked for twenty-two years in the BBC newsroom and has produced six books, the latest being* Against the Flow: Wading through Eastern Europe. *He is married with five children, and his enthusiasms include fishing, playing cricket and attempting to play the piano.*

The Joy of Walking

by ADAM NICOLSON

~

I was twenty-one, in my last year at Cambridge. I was reading English and, like most other English undergraduates in 1979, was floating about with a pretty vapid idea of what might happen next.

That April I went home for a weekend. A publisher who has since died, Christopher Falkus, a friend of my father's, came to lunch. 'What are you doing?' he asked.

'Reading *Finnegans Wake*,' I said, which wasn't really true.

'And what do you like doing?'

'Walking,' I said.

'Well, why don't you write a book about it?'

'OK,' I said, 'I'd love to.'

I remember the hot, winy atmosphere of the dining room, and that wonderful feeling, of something suddenly opening, of your life beginning to slip without warning into a vision of the future. No great announcement or fanfare, just a gentle easing into the sunshine, like the point where the stillness of a loch begins its acceleration into the running of the river, an infinitesimal shift from still to mobile, a change without boundaries, a heavy sliding over of the water into life and movement.

I left Cambridge with a rucksack on my back and walked 2,500 miles across this country in the next eighteen months. In my flat in London I wallpapered my workroom with maps of the British Isles and on them drew the thin, wriggly lines of my own slow journeys across the face of the country. It was like a love affair, and the country my mistress. I carried my tent on my back, a beautiful piece of space-age technology called an Ultimate Equipment Solo Packer 2, which weighed a pound and a half, and I slept wherever I felt like. I became supremely fit. I read vastly about geology and geography and local history. I hardly spoke to anyone. It was too private for that. A reviewer of the book I eventually wrote said that it was as if I had walked through a country in which a cluster of neutron bombs had been dropped: no apparent damage to the buildings or landscape but not a person to be seen. I took that as a compliment. Occasionally a friend came with me. 'Is this really what you do day after day?' one of them said, incredulous after a morning. 'Why?'

And what was the answer to that? I said – and I don't remember where these words came from – that I liked 'making the kicked clover and buttercups hiss with the edges of my shoes', that I liked going, just the process of going, the simplicity and the self-sufficiency of it, and that I loved getting to know the earth like this. Was that enough of an answer? 'What are you running away from?' someone asked me. I couldn't say then but I think I can now. I was escaping from all the abstractions and all the delayed gratifications of modern life. My walking, driven by a blind and powerful appetite, was nothing but drinking in long, strong draughts of the immediate and the real for which, at least intuitively, I knew I had a desperate thirst. In many ways, I'm thirsty still.

> ADAM NICOLSON *is a journalist and writer. His first book, published in 1981, was* The National Trust Book of Long Walks.

The Pleasure of Litter-picking
by VALERIE GROVE

It's seven years since my son Oliver found a litter-picking stick in the street, and handed it to me on my birthday, saying, 'Stop complaining about litter – do something.'

At first I was almost furtive. I would go out with my stick, hoping nobody was watching, fill a plastic bag with crisp packets, bottles and cans, and dump it in a bin. I felt like an eccentric old bat, but was consoled by the fact that where'er I walked became a pleasanter place.

Now I feel quite differently. I am brazen, flagrant. Every day, a passer-by will stop, smile and say 'Thank you!' or 'That's a very noble task you are performing' or 'How very public-spirited of you'. I have a stock reply: 'But I'm doing it for ME,' I say.

Yes, I am. Instead of fretting and fulminating about the disfigured greenswards and woodlands of our neighbourhood, I have personally transformed them. The disused railway line behind our road – 'the 'Parkland Walk', a nature reserve, with three hundred species of wildflower and twenty-two kinds of butterfly – was permanently rubbish-strewn until I came along.

The year I started, the *Evening Standard* published the results of a MORI poll: Which social annoyance most affects our quality of life? At the top – higher than graffiti, vandalism, traffic noise, drunkenness, drug dealers and, difficult neighbours – came litter.

Yet householders, even in affluent enclaves, with market values upwards of £2 million, seem happy to wade through polystyrene cartons at their gates and up their driveways, or park the wheels of their Porsches over crushed plastic bottles. I know what they think – 'I didn't drop it, so I shan't pick it up' or 'It's the council's job'. Isn't pride weird? They're blockheads.

My son's prep school headmaster gave the boys a memorable little mantra on their first day. Ten words long, he said, and no word is more than two letters: 'If it is to be, it is up to me.' Rather brilliant, I thought, and jolly useful. It's the antithesis of 'Why should I?' and it soothes the savage breast. Pick litter up – it's gone in a trice. It doesn't hurt.

That's the great epiphanic moment, when you realise that it's not demeaning, but uplifting. Like the person who clatters the dishes while others lounge on sofas (all mothers know this), you score the Brownie points, you are the queen bee, they are the drones, sloths and low creeping creatures. As Jocasta Innes said in her book, *Home Time*, whoever minds most about household mess has to be the one who deals with it. Litter may be, like housework, a Sisyphean task. But the chores of life are the comforts of life, indoors or out.

In an hour away from my desk, when others swan off to expensive and indulgent lunches, I am fulfilling four impulses: (1) narcissism – keeping fit; (2) work – listening to the radio on my digital personal stereo, for my *Oldie* wireless column; (3) duty – exercising a lively dog; and (4) altruism – improving our environment. And not a penny piece spent! Just count the endorphins unleashed.

My first litter-stick was a Standard Easi-Reach Gripper. I now have a superior Classic Gripper, bought on-line for £11.99. It has a smart, comfortable yellow handle, and its gripping is fantastically deft. I can pick up a filter-tip, a rubber band, a paperclip, a ring-pull, a needle. And it could be brandished menacingly at muggers – an untested additional use, but who would dare attack me with my stick with the metal claw?

Victory is there, if we take arms, or grippers.

Mrs Thatcher was once (absurdly) photographed in St James's Park, picking up crisp packets. She said how embarrassing it was, bowling along the road from Heathrow with a visiting head of state, looking out on a motorway whose embankments are festooned with rubbish. Richard Branson was appointed 'litter czar'. In 1988 there was to be a London-wide offensive backed by on-the-spot fines. Mrs Bottomley, environment minister, proclaimed her strategy: 'We must encourage a climate of opinion in which litter dropping is seen as offensive, boorish and selfish behaviour.' Tidy Britain Year (1990) came and went. All quite pointless.

You can't change uncivilised behaviour. 'Take your litter home with you' never did catch on. The only thing you can do is deal with it yourself. We've all been to Disneyland, where roller-skating litter-pickers in white space-suits dart about keeping everything spotless. And every year at Wimbledon the All-England Club shows what can be achieved with purple litter-bags on every railing. In Germany it's the law to clean up outside homes and shops. In Madrid, the streets are scoured nightly. In Singapore you get arrested for dropping a fag-end. Our litter laws are ignored: but every household could be supplied with a gripper stick along with its wheelie-bin. Or get one for yourself, and keep it by the front door. *If it is to be, it is up to me*. I promise you, picking up litter is good for morale: positive, heartening, deeply satisfying. And free.

VALERIE GROVE *is a writer for* The Times, *a mother of four and a biographer whose latest book is* So Much To Tell: The Story of Kaye Webb, Puffin's Greatest Editor.

Foraging for Mushrooms
by SAM KILEY

Mirrored light from the estuary bounces around in the tops of the trees. Slight depressions in the sandy soil hold enough damp for small soft islands of moss. Clusters of bracken crowd around the trees, between them a springy carpet of pine needles and birch mulch.

It's not my wood. I love it no less for that. In the late autumn my heart skitters with anticipation on the one-minute walk from my home. If there has been plenty of rain, followed by a blanket of warm, I know I'll find.

Impossible to see at a glance, young Bay Boletus poke their brown heads through the decaying mulch which hide their baobab stems. As the eye learns to pick the suede of the boletus from the leaf litter they pop into vision. The basket begins to fill.

I giggle and leap between the fungi and slice them away from the woodland with a specially curved mushroom knife. I am in delight. Melissa will be pleased.

The vulgar fecund perfume of a cauliflower fungus threads into my head. They are huge and white and make me sick with excitement.

And outside my house an old oak is poking out great reddish-orange tongues of Chicken of the Woods – the most exquisite of the gifts from our trees. I have enough now for a feast.

Chicken of the Woods fried with bacon. Earwigs and beetles knocked out, the cauliflower fungus chopped into white wine and cream. Boletus is dried on the radiator to slip into pasta.

I can see pigeon barrelling in to roost, and pulling my boots back on I giggle some more and head out with a gun. I am happy, a bumpkin in the bounty.

Educated at Lady Margaret Hall, Oxford, SAM KILEY *is an award-winning war correspondent and the author of the critically acclaimed book about the conflict in Afghanistan,* Desperate Glory.

Painting the Landscape
by MERLIN WATERSON

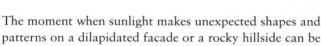

The moment when sunlight makes unexpected shapes and patterns on a dilapidated facade or a rocky hillside can be the reward for hours of reconnaissance; and recompense for all the frustrations that are part of painting out-of-doors. My favourite subjects tend to be abandoned buildings in deserted countryside, sometimes reached after a long walk that may well fail to find the right viewpoint or sufficient shade. Often an unforgiving sun reaches too soon into the protective corner of a courtyard or finds a break in the foliage of a tree and glares back from the paper or canvas. But these setbacks are all part of an activity that is fascinating precisely because each picture is an exploration that can end in exhilaration or failure. There are times when the effort to capture a particular visual experience in a painting seems to be a way of laying hold on reality itself.

Plenty of other recreations involve patient observation. There are similarities with fishing a tranquil stretch of river, when the long-awaited rise ruffles the surface, or there are signs of movement under a shady bank. The bird-watcher experiences a comparable thrill at a rare sighting. But for me nothing quite matches the excitement of sunlight recomposing the subject of a painting. As Constable once told a lady surprised that he was painting a building she thought unattractive: 'No, Madam, there is nothing ugly; *I never saw an ugly thing in my life*: for let the form of an object be what it may – light, shade, and perspective will always make it beautiful.'

Constable is a model for any aspiring painter. His early drawings are clumsy and unimpressive, but as he filled notebook after notebook with sketches, so his proficiency and confidence grew. He took to painting small rapid oil studies out of doors, capturing the effects of sun after rain, of scudding clouds or patches of light racing across the sea. The hesitant late developer became a master of observation and eventually a brilliant and revolutionary painter.

For *plein-air* painting in all weathers, particularly with the constantly changing light of the English climate, the oil sketch is my preferred medium. I used to pack a heavy easel in a rucksack, but I have recently taken to using a light wooden box, called a *pochade*, which can be perched on one's knees. When open, the lid acts as a support for a small wooden panel and protects it once completed.

Why does one devote so much time and effort to an activity which often serves only to fill the waste-paper basket? Even Turner said towards the end of his life that he felt he was only just beginning to learn how to paint. One answer is given in Winston Churchill's perceptive little book, *Painting as a Pastime*, in which he writes: 'I know of nothing which, without exhausting the body, more entirely absorbs the mind.' The book was first published in 1948 and has the admirable aim of not presuming 'to explain how to paint, but only how to get enjoyment'. Churchill explains that he wrote it out of a sense of gratitude: he was struggling to come to terms with his crushing defeat at the polls in 1945 and 'painting came to my rescue'. He concluded: 'Happy are the painters, for they shall not be lonely. Light and colour, peace and hope, will keep them company to the end, or almost to the end, of the day.'

❧ MERLIN WATERSON *is the author of* The Servants' Hall *and* The National Trust: The First Hundred Years. *He worked for the Trust for over thirty years, latterly as Director of Historic Properties.*

A Fascination with Soil
by CHARLES DOWDING

❧

In my gardens I am fortunate enough to enjoy daily contact with healthy, growing, edible plants. They look after me as much as I look after them. Sometimes, ashamedly, I carry a bad mood with me into the garden, yet it always turns to wonder at the sight of high-quality growth, leaves full of shining lustre, all miraculously appearing out of soil!

What is this brown stuff that somehow has the ability both to nurture plants and provide all the growth that sustains us?

My first contact with soil's amazing power came from a morning's weeding when I was working as a maintenance man for a distant hotel. I had injured my knee and could not put any weight on one leg, so was sent to the vegetable garden, where I spent the entire morning pulling weeds on my hands and knees. Then, upon standing up at lunchtime, to my surprise and amazement, the knee was healed.

Since then I have become a professional gardener and notice more and more the ability of well-tended soil to bestow wonderful qualities on plants. These glowing plants can then inspire and uplift visitors to the garden, as well as affording meals of high quality.

Food is beautiful, all the more so when it is still growing. One of the most attractive sights I can imagine is a garden of varied vegetables, growing healthily in well-tended soil, at almost any time of year. And while admiring them, the imagination can roam freely amongst all those fine flavours.

Vegetable gardens also change rapidly, from day to day and from season to season. Each time of year has its own beautiful highlights, from multicoloured salads in spring and flowering beans in summer, to feathery carrots and dark red radicchios in autumn, and then a surprisingly wide range of plants to be sculpted in outline by winter's frost.

An important part of appreciating all this beauty is one's contact with it through tending the plants and soil. Food gardens above all need constant attention, and Kipling's verse from *Glory of the Garden* is nowhere more apt:

> Our England is a garden, and such gardens are
> not made
> By singing: – 'Oh, how beautiful!' and sitting
> in the shade.

The trick is to be organised enough that certain unavoid-able chores do not become too demanding of time. Weeding is often the main culprit, and if weeds are allowed to grow out of hand, the creative pleasure of tending plants is much diminished. My approach to weeds is extremely strict: I pull them tiny. None are allowed to seed and so the soil stays immaculately clean, which is a further uplifting sight for the gardener. Gardening is then a pleasure and does not turn into work.

This is all made easier by correct treatment of soil. My garden is not dug and there are few weeds to pull. Experience of many years suggests that soil really dislikes being tilled and responds to any such painful disturbance by growing a carpet of weeds, which serve to re-cover the cultivated soil as well as helping it to recover, in a healing sense.

Vegetables that are asked to grow in undisturbed soil have a different quality to those in dug soil, especially in the first half of the year, while the dug soil is still regaining its health.

I watch this process unfold every year on four experimental beds, of which two are dug and two are left undug. The extra lustre of salad leaves and spinach growing in the undug beds makes me wonder to what extent the immeasurable aspects of quality in growth that define a successful garden are related to the invisible part of creation that lies under our feet.

Whatever the answer, it gives me enormous pleasure, while spreading compost on top of the soil, to imagine how it is welcomed by all the soil life coming to be nourished by it. Then to sow and plant into the surface compost, and be awed by the gorgeous plants which develop.

And finally, to taste that quality.

∿ CHARLES DOWDING *grows salad leaves and vegetables on two acres of undug beds near Bruton in Somerset; all are sold locally. He has also written two books on growing vegetables, and gives lectures and runs day courses at the farm.*

Working Wood

by ADAM HART-DAVIS

~

One day in 1999 I went to Westonbirt Arboretum to see Henry Russell starting work on the construction of the oak barn which has become the visitor centre. Great oak trees were lying around, and Henry was doing heroic things with an axe. Later I got to know him and his brother John much better when they made a series of magnificent oak props for the television series *What the Romans Did for Us*. I had immense fun squeezing grapes in their wine press, and especially pumping water with their fantastic water wheel at a gold mine in South Wales.

Also at Westonbirt on that day was Gudrun Leitz, demonstrating the use of a pole lathe. I was allowed to have a try, and was instantly hooked; in fact, Gudrun changed my life. She runs green woodwork courses in the woods near Hereford, and I have been to one of these courses almost every year since then. I have found no better way to enjoy a mildly strenuous and yet utterly relaxing week, far from phones and email.

The courses take place in a clearing deep in Clissett Wood, far from any building or source of power. Nine or ten punters, of mixed age, sex and ability, hack away at their wood under a huge awning, surrounded by trees and light. For those staying onsite, in huts or tents, there is a new shower room and a charming compost toilet, with a warm wooden seat and lovely views across the valley. Every day a vast vegetarian lunch appears on the home-made table, and everyone exchanges news of triumphs and disasters with their projects.

The real joy, however, lies in working with the wood. Gudrun is a superb teacher, and within hours the novice can master the use of the basic tools – the splitting axe, the side-axe, the shave horse and draw-knife, and above all the pole lathe, with its roughing-out gouge, flat chisel, and skew chisel. The lathe demands complete concentration, and coordination of both hands, while standing on one foot; the only sound, apart from the birdsong and occasional whoops of joy or frustration from the others, is the gentle *ssshhh . . . ssshhh . . .* of the chisel paring away the wood. Gradually the plan becomes a set of physical objects; with much care and rescuing of mistakes they come together, and finally the chair materialises. Not only does the work take me far from my normal life, but I return there with a useful object.

On Gudrun's courses I have made three chairs, a bench for two, a couple of tables, and several other bits and pieces, but more importantly I have caught the bug. Here at home I built a saw-horse from recycled fence rails. Then, with Gudrun's encouragement, I made my own pole lathe and shave horse – all from recycled timber – and using them I have made two tables, six stools and several egg cups, spatulas, spirtles (porridge stirrers) and wonky pencils, all of which have made lovely Christmas presents. Meanwhile Santa brought me some beautiful wood-carving tools, and I am progressing to spoons and signs.

One of the joys of this woodwork is that it costs almost nothing. True, the tools cost money, but you have to buy them only once, and they should last for a lifetime. What is more, I inherited a few and bought several of the others in sales for a pound or two each. They need regular sharpening, but that in itself is another set of intriguing skills, which I am gradually learning from Gudrun and others, from books, and by practice.

Working with wood has become a major part of my life; it is a simple pleasure, and a continual learning process, and I am a better person for it.

✎ ADAM HART-DAVIS *is a scientist, writer, photographer and broadcaster, but was born and raised in the countryside, and has begun to rediscover some country roots; his passion for simple technology has led him to the joys of green woodwork.*

Welsh Rain

by STEPHEN BAYLEY

They say Cardiff has 89 per cent relative humidity in December and January. This is surely evidence of modesty as a national trait. There have been many times in my experience when the volume of wetness in the Welsh air greatly exceeds 100 per cent.

The Welsh have a single word for rain: *glaw*. Given the nation's practical and spiritual engagement with wetness, it would be tempting to make linguistic comparisons with the Inuit and their reputedly many words for the snow that is their own unfortunate milieu. But that's a fiction. We owe it to the anthropologist Franz Boas, who in a 1911 paper claimed that the Eskimo (as he erroneously and derogatorily called them) had four distinct words for snow. Like a compression wave, this figure eventually grew to more than a hundred. Steven Pinker explained, 'counting generously', experts can in fact 'come up with about a dozen'.

Despite the poverty of the language, the Welsh have many types of rain. But in any case, it is not so much a matter of precipitation as a national state of mind. The sheer materiality of Welsh Rain is a thing of as much profound and magical wonder as *The White Book of Rhydderch*. I once phoned a man called Llewellyn who was in possession of local knowledge about a destination that I was attempting to reach by road in the middle of winter. Needing to plan a route, I asked about the weather. 'It's raining up,' he told me. Welsh Rain requires its own Admiral Beaufort to calibrate, classify and describe its amazing variety.

Possibly the wettest part of a very wet country is Pistyll-y-Rhaedr which lies at the end of the small road out of Llanrhaedr-ym-Mochnant. The landscape – and indeed people – around here gave George Borrow a lot of the more robust and challenging material for *Wild Wales*, his mega-lomaniac travelogue of 1862. I have stood at the base of the thunderous vertical torrent that is Europe's tallest water-fall while heavy mist swirls around. And through the heavy mist, unbelievably, comes stabbing rain to add yet more wetness to the waterfall's noteworthy splashback. Two oiled sweaters, a leather jacket plus a Barbour and you still do not feel entirely secure. But that, of course, is part of the sensation.

The Welsh have a positive – indeed, greedy – genius for melancholy. Gwyn Thomas once said, 'There are still parts of Wales where the only concession to gaiety is a striped shroud.' There is a special sense of Wales, an overwhelming *genius loci*, that rain positively enhan-ces. The wet weather can be, if you have a mind to appreciate it, a pleasure in itself. After all, since it is inevitable, why not enjoy it?

Over the past thirty years, STEPHEN BAYLEY's *exhibitions, books, articles and his Design Museum have helped frame the international concept of design. His wife has a house in Wales.*

Window Gazing

by LIZ ELLIOT

As children in the early 1950s, my brother and I were allowed to take our bicycles only as far as various landmarks deemed to be within a safe distance from home. One such spot was a small, disused or bombed-out foundry which stood dilapidated, dismal and forgotten behind a pair of wooden gates, its only claim to a previous life of any distinction represented by the two tall oriel windows that remained, defiant and glassless, at either end of the building. Made of iron and divided into a column of small squares topped by intact, delicate fans of iron, they imprinted themselves on my visual memory, a romantic and graphic image of a life that might have been, which has stayed with me ever since.

Windows stare you in the face and are the elemental part of the attraction of any building. From the glory of the Rose window at Chartres, the half-moon glass that sends great shafts of light into New York's Grand Central Station, the graceful symmetry of a Georgian window, or those of the beautifully restrained bronzed frontage of Mies van de Rohe's Seagram building, they all imbue in me a feeling of satisfaction and calm, better than any tranquil-liser.

The basis for this formal beauty comes from math-ematical principles, the Golden Section, a ratio denoted by the Greek character phi and used by civilisations from the Egyptians and the Greeks on. Described by Plato as a line divided into two sections, so that the ratio of the short portion to the longer is equal to the ratio of the longer to the whole, this deceptively simple equation relates to so much of what surrounds us – art, music and, above all, nature – that it is difficult to establish whether we use the measurement consciously, or whether it is something that we sense unconsciously, and which, since the brain is the best computer there is, we know instinctively to be right and, more important, to feel right.

So either at the moment of seeing a building from afar, its long windows catching the light, or in happy contem-plation when gazing out of a window that is perfectly measured and placed, it is the proportions that ease my mind, that invite me to look further and admire the building. Proportions, and an inexplicable passion for deli-cate glazing bars. These vertical and horizontal lines define a window – large slabs of glass appear blank and uninviting without the dividing and outlining of each pane – and the finer the dividing line, the more delicate the window, and the more distinguished the building as a whole.

I am not alone in my obsession. Last year, the Royal Academy held an exhibition of paintings by the Danish painter Vilhelm Hammershoi. Much influenced by the seventeenth-century Dutch masters, his paintings are mono-chromatic illustrations of interiors, using the vertical and horizontal lines of a window as a symbol of connection to, and protection from, the outside world. The view without is scarcely visible, so that it is the simplicity and geometric order of the window that dominates the picture, bringing a peace and order to the whole.

Sadly, it appears that the manufacturers of modern, mass-produced commercial windows have never heard of – or felt – the unconscious pull of the Golden Section; their products, no doubt for reasons of security and economy, are manufactured in such a way as to make them heavy, inelegant and out of proportion, to the detriment of much of modern housing and, by extension, to us, the passers-by. In this country, since the 1950s, buildings have sprung up, with no apparent input from a human being, which have distorted our cities and dwarfed the beauties that have gone before. So close your eyes to these modern monstrosities and instead seek out the quieter, more researched example, because as a form of therapy window-mania is surprisingly successful and completely free. I recommend it.

✎ LIZ ELLIOT *is Editor-at-Large for* House & Garden.

Amaryllis

by ANTONIA FRASER

~

'To sport with Amaryllis in the shade . . .' What Milton
had in mind in *Lycidas* was indeed a simple pleasure, since
he contrasted this kind of innocent pastime with the need
for the ambitious life in which 'fame is the spur'. I too
enjoy sporting with Amaryllis in the shade, but I have a
rather different way of doing it. I plant the bulbs in the
autumn as shade begins to deepen in order to enjoy them
in splendour from Christmas onwards. (Incidentally,
whether influenced by Milton or not, I have always preferred
the melodic but inaccurate name of Amaryllis to the official name of Hippeastrum. It's true that the latter means
'horseman's star' in Greek but somehow a rustic shep-
herdess is more sympathetic.)

For me growing Amaryllis offers a triple delight. First
of all there is the enjoyment of choosing things called Mont
Blanc, Apple Blossom and Fairy Tale, which, having been
plunged into a pot, actually do come up looking remark-
ably like their photographs in the catalogue. Last year, for
example, I chose Liberty, a striking bright clear red designed
especially for Christmas – well, who wouldn't choose

Liberty at Christmas if not from Christmas? The tall, strong multi-flowering stems beat all the other Christmas decorations. (Red amaryllis have had some distinguished admirers: Winston Churchill particularly loved painting them in their pots, which he could do indoors when the weather was bad.)

Then there is the pleasure of the fact that Amaryllis do come up, right up, following a really simple planting process, and never fail. I have literally never had a bulb that failed me over fifty years, which is more than I can say for any of my other gardening efforts. Furthermore, the bulbs like the same life as I do: liquid refreshment, heat and light; there is none of this furtive concealment in the dark for six weeks, which means that long-forgotten bulbs sometimes get excavated by the cat.

Lastly there is the perennial thrill of showing them off in the drawing-room with that casual line: 'Yes, I really did grow them all myself. It's simple.' And as a matter of fact it is: the results are gigantic in return for modest labour, which must be the hallmark of all the best pleasures.

PS But as a show-off I did once meet my comeuppance when a canny guest entered the room, saw the array of flowers I had grown, realised what I must have been boasting about and said loudly, if untruthfully, 'I'm so glad that all the flowers I sent you have arrived.'

ANTONIA FRASER'S *most recent book is* Must You Go?: My Life with Harold Pinter.

PART FIVE

The Pleasures of the Table

Bread and Cheese

by A. C. GRAYLING

How many factors make a good dish? Is it the freshness and fineness of the ingredients plus the skill of the chef, or is it these combined with the appetite of the eater? High cuisine throughout history has almost exclusively been for the rich, at least many of whom had, precisely because of their wealth, little need to exert themselves physically. As a result the work of prompting and exciting their appetites had to be done by piquant sauces and the visual splendour of dishes they were served.

Thinking of jaded palates and surfeited digestions brings to mind the old saying, 'The poor must walk to get meat for their stomachs, but the rich must walk to get stomach for their meat.' And in that lies a clue. For the ingredient that makes even the simplest fare taste like ambrosia is hunger resulting from exercise. A long walk in the country – a long walk in sunshine through beautiful country, over hills or along a winding coastline, with views and vistas and a light cooling breeze in one's face – will make a king's feast out of two of the most basic ingredients of human diet, and will turn cold water into nectar.

The two ingredients in question are bread and cheese. Imagine settling down on a tree stump with a view, after three or so hours of enjoyable walking, and getting out a sandwich made of fresh crusty buttered bread and a slice of cheddar. Such embellishments as pickles, tomato and lettuce are very good too, but in the envisioned circumstances they are not essential. The bread and cheese by itself is better than the hundred dishes that grim old Empress Ci Xi was served every night by the lake in the Forbidden City, and a bottle of water tastes better than the longest-stored fine wines of the cellars at Versailles.

I remember a moment of epiphany on the subject of cheese sandwiches. It was on the coast path between Lulworth and Weymouth, near Ringstead, on the cliff called White Nothe. This section of the 12-mile journey is for hardier walkers, the crowds having turned back at Durdle Dor, so it is possible to unpack one's sandwiches there in peace, and to sit gazing along the wide sweep of coastline it commands. It was sunny and warm, a perfect day in late May, and I was hungry. After a few gulps of water I bit into my sandwich with eager relish, expecting it to taste good – only to be bowled over by how very, very good it tasted: extra good, superlatively good, good beyond the resources of poetry to describe, and all because I was so hungry and the bread was excellent and the cheese even more so. By a multiplier of factors – scene, hunger, ingredients – something like a gustatory miracle resulted, and I looked at the cheese sandwich in my hand, an arc bitten out of it shaped like the theatre of Epidaurus, and wondered how something so simple could taste so divine.

There are people, I am sure, who go on long walks up hills and deep into valleys for the particular purpose of working up an appetite for their cheese sandwiches. Recently I retraced the steps of William Hazlitt on his 1798 journey from Shropshire to visit Wordsworth and Coleridge in Somerset, and therefore had plenty of opportunities for cheese sandwiches – atop the Long Mynd, on the eastern slopes of the Malverns, on the footpaths between Bridgenorth and Nether Stowey, among the Quantocks' deep romantic chasms and forests as ancient as the hills. How good they tasted, every time! For once the magic has begun it never ends.

The recipe is very simple, but the key is that the bread must be crusty, the butter lightly salted, and the cheddar, whether mild, medium or strong, suited to taste. It's medium for me. And although a bottle of water is all that one needs in place of nectar or Chablis, it has to be admitted that a thermos of tea for afterwards makes an incomparable finish. It's not rocket science, or Michelin three-star; in the right circumstances it's better than the latter.

I have a copy of a Chinese print showing a mandarin sitting at the sliding window of his house overlooking a fine view, while his servant tends a kettle in the next room. The caption says, 'The Mandarin Wu preparing himself to enjoy his tea.' The sentiment is wonderful. Preparing oneself to enjoy one's cheese sandwich is a bit more active – and the better for it – but no less aesthetic.

⤛ A. C. GRAYLING *is Professor of Philosophy at Birkbeck College, University of London. He has written and edited many books on philosophy and other subjects.*

A Soothing Recipe

by YOTAM OTTOLENGHI

The last person you'd want to ask about the little joys in life that could bring serenity and inner calm in the midst of contemporary madness would be me. Being an outright workaholic, the type that gets up and falls asleep to the sound of computer keys clicking, someone who feels some comfort upon completing a project (be it a single recipe or a recipe book), but only for a split of a moment, followed by morose pangs of guilt for not doing something useful of purposeful – you'd run a million miles away from me if not-ever-being-able-to-slow-down was a name of an infectious common disease. This is me and I am, by now, fully accustomed to myself.

I guess this makes me the perfect victim of our age, a symbol of a human condition that is out of balance and out of sorts, a living signpost for the wrong way to happiness. But, miraculously, I survive and, believe it or not, I am actually able to sustain a reasonable quality of life. I manage to do this by having the fortune of a profession that offers the ultimate escape – cooking.

I don't cook all the time, not necessarily even every day, but I cook often enough to encounter moments that are calmer than any kind of meditation has ever given me. I can stand picking herb leaves or whisking egg whites without any sense of time gone by. I can delve into shaping little meatballs or stuffing pastry cases, totally oblivious to the external world that, in any other circumstance, would suck me in in a flash. I flee into a state of detachment and tranquillity, and this is the ultimate source of my sanity.

Try it.

Fried Rice Cakes
with Creamed Leeks and Egg

SERVES FOUR

1 tsp saffron strands
400 g cooked rice of any variety
100 g diced Gruyère
2 tbsp olive oil, plus extra for frying the cakes
3 leeks, trimmed and cut into 1 cm thick slices
250 ml vegetable stock
100 ml double cream
2 tbsp chopped tarragon
5 free-range eggs
Salt and freshly crushed black peppercorns

Mix the saffron with about a tablespoon of boiling water. Leave to infuse for a couple of minutes and then stir this into the rice. Also add the Gruyère to the rice and season it well with salt and pepper.

Next, heat up the olive oil in a large frying pan and fry the leeks for 3 minutes on high heat to give them colour. Add the stock, cream and plenty of crushed black pepper-corns. Cook on a slow simmer for about 10 minutes until the leeks are soft and the sauce is thick. Season with salt to taste and keep warm; stir in the tarragon just before serving.

Add 1 egg to the rice and stir well. Pour a tiny amount of olive oil into a large non-stick frying pan and place on medium heat. With a spoon take some of the rice mix and press it down into the hot oil to create 4 flat cakes, about 1 centimetre thick and 7 centimetres in diameter. Fry them until they turn crispy and brown, about 4 minutes on each side. Continue to make another 4 cakes, transfer to absorbent paper and keep warm.

Fry 4 eggs in the same pan and sprinkle them with salt and pepper. Place 2 cakes per person on serving plates and top with creamed leeks. Place the fried eggs on top and serve, peacefully.

⮞ YOTAM OTTOLENGHI *is a London-based chef and restaurateur. His food is best described as sunny and bears the strong influences of growing up in the Middle East (Israel) to a family of European background (Italy and Germany). He writes a weekly vegetarian column for the* Guardian *and is the author of two books.*

The Great Offal Lunch
by MATTHEW FORT

❧

Some years ago I was lamenting to two of my brothers that, among many other tribulations, we were never allowed to eat offal in our respective homes. When we were growing up offal was a staple of the Fort table: a simple pleasure. But now our extended families shared the contemporary revulsion towards such things as sweetbreads, heart, liver or kidneys cooked in their fat, and these splendid foods had consequently disappeared from the menu.

'Why don't we organise an offal lunch?' suggested one brother. 'You know chefs, Matty,' said the other. 'Surely you could persuade one of them to cook something offally for us.' And so the Great Offal Lunch came about.

It had to be lunch. Supper has its place, to sustain one after a day at the coal face; and dinner has a certain social cachet. But lunch, well, lunch has a flexibility, a generosity, an ease that the other meals lack. Whether at home or in a restaurant, it breaks the day just when you're getting bored of it. It refreshes the spirit as well as the body. As Aldous Huxley put it, 'A man may be a pessimistic determinist before lunch and an optimistic believer in the will's freedom after it.' That you might say, is the heart of the matter.

These days, of course, the mere mention of sweetbreads, heart, liver and kidneys causes people to shudder and look at you oddly, and as for brain, tripe, testicles and all the rest, suggest a feast of those and even your nearest and dearest tend to treat you as if you were suggesting eating a favourite aunt or dog.

This is absurd. Offal is the animal, pure and simple, its essence, its quiddity. Celebrate offal, and you celebrate the animal in its entirety. Ignoring, for a moment, the moral considerations of rearing an animal for your pleasure, and then throwing a good deal of it away, the fact is that offal is the perfect modern dietary food: healthy, low in fat, high in vitamins and minerals, cheap and, above all, delicious. It has taste and texture; it can stand up for itself in hand-to-hand combat with the most stonking of sauces; but it is also mild-mannered enough to tango gracefully in partnership with the most dulcet of partners.

In 1999, I was inveigled to take our custom to Le Gavroche, a place of imperturbable grace and urbanity, and ineffable cooking. That's when and where the Great Offal Lunch, always held in early December, became a proper ritual. And so began one of the happiest eating rituals of my life – the essence, the paragon, of lunch.

When we first sat down together, we realised that this was in all probability the first time we had all sat down together, just us, with no parents, aunts, uncles, cousins, spouses, children or friends to clutter the spaces in between. Conversation flowed then, as it has flowed at each lunch ever since, like the confluence of many streams: funny, diverse, diverting, warm, affectionate.

And the food? *Tête de veau ravigote à la façon de Fernand Point*; *petite salade de crêtes et rognons de coq*; *miel et moutarde de Meaux*; *croustillant d'andouillette et oreilles de porc*; *pieds de porc farcis aux rognons*; *beignets de cervelle de veau*; *tripes à la Niçoise*. We've delighted in ear (pig), nose (pig) and throat (hake). We've meditated on the qualities of liver and lites; heart and fries; tongue and trotter. Chitterlings and gizzards have called for a nicety of judgement that Plato or Socrates would have recognised. Over the years, there are few parts of lamb, sheep, beef or poultry that the kitchen and creativity of Michel Roux and his team have not honoured. Their skill and inspiration has never faltered, and our resolution to eat whatever the courteous and charming service has placed in front of us has never wavered.

Lunch begins at 12.30 and finishes at – well, when we finish. We arrive sober and depart glowing, replete with that sense of well-being that comes from having been well fed, filled with cheer and happiness, humming with sunny discourse and familial concord. As the long-forgotten Charles Stuart Calverley put it: 'Fate cannot touch me: I have dined today.' Of course, he meant lunched.

❧ MATTHEW FORT *is an author, journalist, television presenter, cook and* bon viveur.

The Morning Sun and Cornflakes

by ARTEMIS COOPER

The dining room smells of wood polish and damp curtains, and the beams and red-tiled floor have tilted gently over the centuries until no straight line remains. It's very early, but already the round oak table is laid with yellow crockery and boxes of cereal – I'd like to think it was the fairies who set it, though I'm old enough to know it was Nanny before she went to bed. Shafts of early sunlight are streaming through the long low window, stirred by the breeze, broken by the transparent green leaves of the hazel that grows just outside. Beyond, the grass is white and silver with dew. This is the sunlight of childhood happiness; the sunlight that greets the first one up, who gets to scrabble through the cornflakes packet to find the free parachutist . . . I'm elbow-deep in scratchy cornflakes before I can feel him. Yes! There he is – careful bringing him up, get all the flakes back in the packet quick before Nanny comes and hope she doesn't notice the crumbs . . .

I sit back to examine my prize, and have to admit that he doesn't look quite as good as he does on the back of the packet. Beside the words EXCITING FREE GIFT!, the parachutist is swinging into the picture in full colour, goggles glinting, his huge yellow parachute taut against a blue sky. What I have in my hand is a moulded lump of grey-green plastic, attached by four tangled strings to a square of polythene. Still, I refuse to be disappointed. He's *mine*, I'm sure I can make him a better parachute, and it's going to be a wonderful day.

~ ARTEMIS COOPER'S *books include* Cairo in the War 1939–1945 *and the biography of Elizabeth David. She is currently writing the biography of Patrick Leigh Fermor.*

Growing Your Own Food

by SARAH RAVEN

It is one of the mysteries of modern life that the greatest pleasures are the simplest and the deepest. In our days of constant busy rushing and intense and varied stimulation, surrounded by crowds of people from one day to the next, it's the things that are opposite to that which are the most precious – and growing your own food ranks pretty highly.

With a productive garden right outside your door you are alive in the world, with eyes, nose, ears and fingers all engaged and connected to the natural. Even if I lived in a high-rise with no garden, I would grow plants for that reason. It drives you back into the soil, back into the seasons – back into the newness and possibilities of spring, the pushing out and abundance of summer, the bounty and slowing down of autumn and the pared-down reduction of the winter. I'd be at sea without that engagement.

Add to that the element of nurturing, the simple pattern of bringing something into life and tending it from germi-nation to harvest. Early in the morning and in the evening I'll go to my propagator bench and see what has come up in the past few hours. I play solitaire, moving seedlings which have emerged from the hot bench on to the cold and sowing more to fill any precious space. Out go some and in come others in an incredibly simple yet satisfying roll.

There's an aesthetic to it all, too: creating a place that is beautiful. Abundance is the key. There's nothing more beautiful, simply for its oomph, than a hugely productive growing machine out there, delivering a steady, constant stream of deliciousness into the kitchen. I love the mix of productive plants; potatoes, parsnips and rhubarb, robust, dense and chunky; carrots, asparagus, herbs and salads, all fine-looking and more delicate; and the vertical climbers of mini pumpkins, climbing beans and peas which break up any monotony at ground level, the tall-growing trees in the wood of productivity. With big, strong splashes of colour from plenty of frames of fragrant sweet peas and Venetian coloured dahlias – both these ornamental plants thrive in rich veg garden soil – you have a vision of paradise.

The scientist in me also loves the experimentation that goes with veg gardening. If I do this, will the plant do that? Many of the plants are on an annual path that is set, but you can affect that by what you do to it. Which is the best moment on your soil to feed – or not – whether to water and where to plant? It's all part of the ever-improving aim of a gardener and I love the tests and trials which go with that.

And there is always something new. Last year I had a wilted green at the River Café – agritti – and loved it, similar in texture but more fragrant in taste than samphire, the wild plant of our coastal mudflats. You can't grow samphire in a garden, but I've managed to find seed and now I am growing agritti. In a restaurant in Holland last summer I made another discovery – metensia – a salad leaf which tastes like an oyster. It's incredible – just a little in a big bowl of salad – and this year I'm trying to grow that, too.

Harvesting – collecting eggs from the chickens, draining honey from the hive, picking tomatoes from the vine – those are the greatest high moments. Sometimes it may feel like a chore, and then the supermarket bag of ready-washed and even chopped veg or salad is a tempting thing. That's fine, but with your own patch, you create a living shop stocked only with the things you love. Walk outside and you can fill your kitchen with your favourite food. I love salad and there's no better salad than I can pick in my garden. As we eat, I know every variety, every leaf, a selection evolved over years, chosen for their different flavours – hot or mild – different shapes, textures and colours to combine into a perfect salad.

And with me – there's no denying it – I love the showing off, the flamboyance, bringing food to the table to be greeted by 'What's that? How amazing. Did you grow it?' That's a good moment to be cherished.

SARAH RAVEN *is a writer, cook, broadcaster and teacher, and an expert on all things to grow, cut and eat from your garden. She runs a mail order company (sarahraven.com) and cooking, flower arranging, growing and gardening courses at the school she set up in 1999 at her farm in East Sussex.*

Home-grown Honey
by MARTHA KEARNEY

❧

Onto warm, home-baked bread fresh from the oven, glistening with unsalted butter sunk deep into the pores of the slice, I pour ribbons of light golden honey, the fragrance of wild flowers just perceptible. That is my fantasy simple pleasure.

The reality is just a touch more complicated. Getting that honey on my teaspoon has meant hours, if not days, of hard labour – and I'm not just talking about the bees. I will have spent the months of winter fretting whether my hive has survived; the spring preventing a swarm and then, if I am very lucky, I will reach the day of extraction in which every floor and surface becomes sticky with honey as I decant the crop into jars.

What do you mean, why not just buy it? Where would be the pleasure in that?

❧ MARTHA KEARNEY *is the presenter of* The World at One *on Radio 4 and* The Review Show *on BBC2.*

Baking with the Children

by ZEINAB BADAWI

~

I travel a lot for work and, even when in London, I often spend long hours in the newsroom or filming, which means I cannot pick up my children from school as often as I would like. I have four children all very close in age – two sons and two daughters – and being reunited with them after a trip away still makes my heart leap.

We live in Hampstead Village in north London – narrow streets, lots of cars, no use trying to drive short distances – so we walk home together, chatting the whole way. When I pick up my youngest son from school, he will often lead me right past the ice-cream van, hoping to persuade me to buy him a screwball, with a bubble-gum at the bottom as a special treat. I sometimes buy myself a special treat, too – a 99 with a flake.

Once the other children are all home I will give them an early supper – usually something I have prepared earlier (in true *Blue Peter* style) – like a salmon dish with pota-toes and vegetables. If it is a Friday and there is no home-work to do that night then I *love* baking with them.

The girls will put on their aprons: jolly affairs, pink and

yellow ones that I got them from Spain a few years ago. My ten-year-old son, Zac, does not mind getting grubby and will pull up a stool to stand on to reach a comfortable height at the kitchen counter. My elder daughter, Sophia, will peel the apples very patiently and efficiently; I hate doing it – and she knows that – so she obliges. Zac slices and cuts up the apples and Hannah mixes the apple pieces in with sugar and blackberries in the dish. Then we weigh the flour, sugar and butter for the crumble on the scale – I bake with a scientist's precision.

The best bit next: we all muck in in turns with our fingers to make the crumble mixture – a very therapeutic experience. Sophia, a good instinctive cook, unlike her mother, will announce wisely that it needs more flour to make it firmer. My eldest son, Joey, will usually pop into the kitchen at this stage to inspect our efforts. Apple and blackberry crumble is his favourite, so he takes a very keen interest in its progress but plays no part in its production.

Once we have all pronounced ourselves happy with the consistency of the mixture, it is carefully loaded on top of the fruit and then I pop the dish into the oven. The sweet smell soon fills the kitchen.

Baking with my children is one of the simplest pleasures in life for me. I wish I could do it more often than I do. The camaraderie, the chatter that is going on the whole time we are preparing our dish simply makes the pressures and strains of everyday life disappear. Crumble cooked, we all sit down together and tuck in, ice cream and cream on hand – true heaven.

➳ ZEINAB BADAWI *has worked in the media for more than two decades. She is the presenter of Britain's only domestic news programme dedicated to international news on television, on BBC4, and works on a variety of other programmes.*

PART SIX

Talking and Ruminating

Conversation versus Discussion
by PEREGRINE WORSTHORNE

❧

Recently I noticed a college advertisement which read as follows: 'If you want to be successful, first learn the art of conversation.' This seemed to me to miss the point: rather as would a Church of England advertisement which said, 'If you want to succeed, first learn to pray.' For just as prayer undertaken for reasons of personal ambition won't get answered, neither will a conversation begun for that end give much pleasure: indeed won't in the true meaning of the word be a conversation at all.

Discussion, however, is another matter, operates in another universe. Discussion is a formal exchange of information between business associates about a particular project or stratagem, conducted usually in a boardroom or a council chamber, while conversation is an informal exchange of ideas and gossip between friends, conducted ideally in a gentleman's club or pub. The former is for work; the latter, essentially, for leisure; not to be indulged in by anybody in a hurry or on the make, which is why, of course – in a world where everybody is in a hurry and on the make – it is very much a dying art. A quotation from the nineteenth-century American writer Henry Thoreau says it all: 'The government of the world I live in,' he wrote, 'was not framed, like that of Britain, in after-dinner conversation over the wine.' Lucky old Britain. Professionals discuss: amateurs, subject to no particular discipline or body of rules – which is very much what journalists in my day were – converse, sharpening their wits by interaction rather than, like Descartes, by just staring gloomily into the fire.

Memory takes me back to the late 1950s, 60s and 70s when I was part of a small group of journalists who tended habitually to come together at about midday in El Vino's, a Fleet Street watering hole where hours were passed informally exchanging ideas and gossip. If anybody thought we were industrially putting our heads together for some journalistic project, they would be greatly mistaken. Lord Beaverbrook, proprietor of the *Daily Express*, was not mistaken. He knew full well we were *conversing*, not *discussing*, which is why he tried to forbid any journalist employed by the *Express* from going to El Vino's. He suspected, quite rightly, that they were not 'on the job' which his papers were paying them for. Nor were they. They were conversing: the best recreational activity known to humankind. The aim was not so much to score goals as to keep the ball in the air. Competitive, argumentative colleagues were kept at arm's length; so were point-scorers. Conversation was an end in itself, served no practical purpose, and it was because journalism was by then about the only way of earning a living that allowed for this bohemian self-indulgence, that we drifted into that *demi-monde* in the first place.

Of course, the greatest conversationalist of all time was Montaigne, the sixteenth-century French nobleman who invented the essay. According to a lovely new biography by Sarah Bakewell, he depended on conversation so much that he would rather have lost his sight than his hearing or speech; to talk, in his view, was better than books. Nor did the talk have to be serious: what he liked best was 'the sharp, abrupt repartee which good spirits and familiarity introduce among friends, bantering and joking wittily and keenly with one another'. Any conversation was good so long as it was kindly spirited and friendly. Contradictions, too, were to be encouraged as they opened up more interesting conversations and helped one to think. Essentially the aim was to cultivate 'a gay and sociable wisdom' – something which modern communication technologies have done nothing to facilitate.

Let me end with a personal confession: as editor of the *Sunday Telegraph*, I was allowed to hold a regular in-house luncheon party, and selfishly I would try to persuade my colleagues and guests to concentrate on one topical subject, so as to help me with my weekly column. It didn't work. My colleagues and guests absolutely refused to cut short their exchange of ideas and gossip. Initially I was frustrated, but very soon began to realise that 'the gaiety and social wisdom' these conversations engendered set my pen flowing far more fluently than would have any insider information that a single subject discussion might have produced.

In other words, if our politicians are ever again to get things right, they should give up the think-tanks and get back to having 'conversations over wine, in a gentleman's club'.

✎ SIR PEREGRINE WORSTHORNE *is former editor of the* Sunday Telegraph.

Gossip

by SARAH SANDS

❧

Naturally, Judi Dench's brave and moving portrayal of Miss Matty Jenkyns in *Cranford* was applauded by critics. Francesca Annis, as Lady Ludlow, also swept up praise. In *Cranford* as in life, stoicism, kindness and *noblesse oblige* reflect well on a person. But if I wanted a really fun evening, I would call on Octavia Pole, the village gossip, marvellously played by Imelda Staunton.

I like the way her eyes widen as she realises the significance of a sighting. Or the way she races to break the news to her friends. There are many unrewarded virtues in a gossip, and one of them is generosity. I am always offended when news of a romance or scandal breaks, and an acquaintance drawls: 'Oh yes, I knew that.' That would be like me saying: 'Oh yes, I knew the sun was going to fall from the sky, but I did not think you were a fit custodian of this information.'

Sharing gossip is a vote of trust and friendship. It is the antithetical impulse to mentioning a fact of stunning dullness, and adding: 'And that is NOT for publication.'

People who make a point of refusing to indulge in gossip

are usually self-righteous bores. (I exempt senior members of the Church and also scientists, who deal in concepts rather than people.) I think more rather than less of a person I hear described as a gossip.

For instance, a panellist on *Any Questions?* mentioned that he would choose to be stuck in a car with Simon Schama, because he was an A-grade gossip. How exciting that a man of such an elevated mind is happy to trade in gossip as well as ideas. I admire Schama but always imagined he might be hard-going in private. Now I think differently. Gossip is what makes a great historian also a delightful dinner companion.

I will always defer to the gossip-free great, such as Lady Thatcher, Tony Benn or Will Hutton, but I don't want to get stuck with them. An easy rule of thumb is whether or not you would like to read their personal diaries, as opposed to listen to a speech. On these terms, I would like to have a drink with Samuel Pepys, and, an unexpected new addition, Antonia Fraser.

Gossip does not have to come from the purest motive but it should not be about self-advancement. I return to the bond of intimacy. One shares gossip as one should share good wine. It is an act of pleasure.

The fallacy about gossip is that it is lowering and distracting from great issues. Politicians are the first to dismiss 'idle tittle-tattle' when what they are afraid of is the illumination. The whole expenses scandal was fundamentally gossip about private behaviour.

Gossip does not have to be about sex, although it helps. It just needs to be surprising, and, at best, outlandish. It is much better if no one has suffered, which is why I find gossip about marriage break-ups awkward. Naturally I like to hear of these things, but the interest is erased by loyalty or indignation or pity.

There is an art to gossip, which is really a moment of memoir. Philosophers of the human heart such as Diana Athill, or heartless but comic diarists such as Alan Clark, tell us more about social history, politics and humanity than autobiographies of public record, which are really only special pleading and dates. I always learn more from a gossip than a prig. Life is a comedy; it is not Hansard.

↬ SARAH SANDS *is Deputy Editor of the London* Evening Standard *and is former Editor of the* Sunday Telegraph *and Deputy Editor and Saturday Editor of the* Daily Telegraph.

Reading Aloud

by RUPERT CHRISTIANSEN

When young Pip writes him a note, Joe Gargery, the illiterate blacksmith in Dickens' *Great Expectations*, finds a physical thrill in recognising the two first letters of his Christian name on the page. 'Why here's three Js and three Os, ands three J-O, Joes, in it, Pip.' Like every child in nursery school, he is making the basic but miraculous link between symbol and sound, through which we all learn to read. Understanding how to internalise it comes much later.

Throughout all cultures, reading aloud was the norm until the late nineteenth century: only an educated elite were ever fluent enough to read silently. Until our own age of mass literacy, the written word did not become a real quantity until it was made flesh in the mouth: a spell did not cast its magic until it was spoken, a liturgy did not become effective until it was sounded, and marks on the page were simply a medium waiting to be verbally interpreted and translated. Lady Macbeth reads the letter from her husband out loud not just for theatrical convenience, but because she can only understand its import by speaking it. The same is true for the dying courtesan Violetta in Verdi's opera *La traviata*: she recites Alfredo's letter over and over again because only thus can she persuade herself of its truth.

The Egyptian and Japanese words for 'to read' – *sdj* and *yomu* – are identical to the words for 'to recite'. Scribes in the ancient world were more valued for their ability to read aloud than to write – they were the equivalent of our audiobooks, if you like. Monks in medieval monasteries sat murmuring the sacred texts to themselves; actors still commit text to their muscular memory by whispering it aloud. Our fluency in skimming and speed-reading is a modern art, and perhaps an evil one.

Reading aloud, this primordial act, gives me the same sensual pleasure that it gave Joe Gargery. I am absolutely terrified and tongue-tied if I am asked to stand up and speak off-the-cuff at a birthday party or on the radio; I was never very much cop in the school play either. But I would happily face a crowd of thousands in Wembley Arena and declaim a Shakespeare sonnet or an essay by Doctor Johnson. It is, in fact, one of the few things in life that I feel I can do well. I'm not proud of much that I've done, but I felt the certainty of achievement when I read the lesson at a memorial service in the chapel of King's College, Cambridge, a poem by Elizabeth Bishop at my wedding, and an encomium at an old friend's funeral. Others might find this nerve-racking – to which I can only say, nerves make one rush and stumble. It's all in the deep firm breathing. Start slowly, and let the pace establish itself in four- or five-word phrases. The bigger the space, the more time you have to take: projecting successfully is more about that than it is about producing unnatural amounts of volume.

Large-scale performance is only one sort of reading aloud: more sociable reading aloud can be equally rewarding. I have been part of a reading group – descendant of the Penny Readings of the Victorian era, so important to the autodidacts of the working class – where four or five of us met over a year to recite the twelve books of Milton's *Paradise Lost*. To anyone who pulls the book off the shelf, and thinks that this epic is daunting, I can only say that you cannot hope to understand the grandeur and genius of the verse until you have savoured it in your own throat like a fine wine.

Yet perhaps the ultimate pleasure in reading aloud is solitary. Open a bottle of wine and light a fire. Take a short story by Henry James – a writer who in his latter years wrote by oral dictation, pacing up and down his study as Miss Theodora Bosanquet took down his words on a stenographic machine – and without embarrassment, begin to give it your voice. The reward is swift: because you can't skate over what on the page look like serpentine sentences, full of sub-clauses and periphrases, you begin to understand not only precisely what James means but also the perfect aptness of his expression. We think there is something naive, primitive even, about reading aloud:

but try this and you will discover that it can give great writing air and life.

✎ RUPERT CHRISTIANSEN *is opera critic for the* Daily Telegraph *and dance critic for the* Mail on Sunday, *as well as the author of* Romantic Affinities, Paris Babylon, The Visitors *and* The Complete Book of Aunts.

A Grasp of Grammar

by SEBASTIAN FAULKS

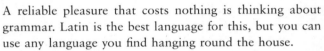

A reliable pleasure that costs nothing is thinking about grammar. Latin is the best language for this, but you can use any language you find hanging round the house.

Think of the lovely line from Virgil: '*Forsan et haec olim meminisse juvabit*', which means roughly, 'Perhaps one day we'll look back even on this and have a laugh.' The pleasure is in the oddness of the two verbs. '*Juvabit*' is the third person singular, impersonal, of the future indicative. '*Meminisse*' is the past infinitive of a defective verb. What a result for old Virgil to have coined an epigram – in verse – from an impersonal and a defective.

The crunchiest grammarian was Tacitus. Think of his description of the useless emperor Galba: '*Capax imperii, nisi imperasset.*' It means, roughly: 'A man all would have thought capable of holding high office with distinction had not his tenure of it proved otherwise.' A sort of Roman Gordon Brown. The joy is in the compression of all that into four words, made possible by the weird '*imperasset*', a contraction of the regular pluperfect subjunctive.

French offers some neat logic in the conjugation of

verbs. For instance, '*J'aurais dû le faire*' translates as 'I ought to have done it'. In English, the sense of the past is expressed by changing 'do' to 'done'; but French transfers the sense of the past to the 'ought' word. This is preferable because the critical moment was a failure not of action but of obligation.

It costs nothing to sit in your favourite chair and turn over these small matters, with a glass of free rainwater in one hand and the sound of birdsong, *gratis*, coming in through the window.

In English, some people puzzle over 'may' and 'might'. If your ear doesn't simply tell you what's right, this might (sic) help:

If may/might forms part of the main verb of the sentence, either can be used; thus both 'I may go to London tomorrow if the sun shines', or 'I might go to London tomorrow if the sun shines' are all right, though the first speaker is more likely to make the trip.

But if may/might is used as an auxiliary to a verb in a dependent clause, then it follows the sequence-of-tenses rule. So if it follows a 'primary' main verb (a verb in the present, future or perfect tense), either may be used, viz.: 'I think this may interest you' or 'I think this might interest you.' But if the main verb is 'historic' (in the imperfect, preterite or pluperfect tense) then *only* 'might' can be used. To say 'I thought this may interest you' is an offence against syntax, while 'I thought of the life we may have had together' implies that the speaker doesn't know whether or not he and the addressee did have a life together.

A lot of people also have trouble with 'I' and 'me', though the rule is dead simple. Use 'I' and 'me' exactly as you would if there were no other person in the sentence. Thus, 'I went to the shops'; 'He gave the book to me.' Then simply put 'John and' in front of either 'I' or 'me'. You wouldn't say 'Me went to the shop' or 'He gave the book to I' – so don't let the addition of 'John and' before the pronoun let you make a fool of yourself.

Or on the current bought/brought confusion, you need to know that 'bought' is the preterite of buy and 'brought' of bring. To say, 'I was bought up in Wales' implies you were sold into slavery as a child, possibly in Swansea.

Of course, I am only an amateur at all this, and a true professional will have spotted the one or two deliberate mistakes in the above.

Isn't life fun? Or as the poet Paul Éluard put it, '*Il n'y a qu'une vie, c'est donc qu'elle est parfaite*' – where an interesting ambiguity attaches to the word '*elle*'.

✍ SEBASTIAN FAULKS *is best known for the French trilogy* The Girl at the Lion d'Or, Birdsong *and* Charlotte Gray. *He is also the author of a triple biography,* The Fatal Englishman; *a small book of literary parodies,* Pistache; *and the novels* Human Traces, Engleby *and* A Week in December.

Cancelled Lunches

by LUCY KELLAWAY

The biggest jolt of pleasure that one human being can give another is to cancel a working lunch. This pleasure can arrive via email, but it is even better by telephone.

The call usually comes at around ten o'clock on the day of the dreaded lunch and the person (or their PA) is on the line uttering the words 'I'm so sorry to do this to you at the last minute', an opener that can only go one joyous way. Due to a sore throat, they say, or delayed flight, something having come up, lunch is off.

'What a shame,' I say, fingers crossed behind my back. 'Hope you feel better soon,' etc. etc. The pleasure of the cancellation made heady both because it is unexpected and because it is illicit: you have to pretend to feel sad, or at any rate inconvenienced, when actually you are experiencing a giddy rush of delight.

Most other pleasures (possibly apart from poisoning bindweed) get less enjoyable as you get older. But the happiness generated by a cancellation goes on growing. I find there are fewer and fewer people I really want to sit across the table from during a working day. Even people you thought it might be good to see when the date was arranged weeks earlier seem unappealing on the day itself.

Instead, the prospect of a few hours to oneself, in which to work, be idle, or be as misanthropic as one likes, seems very heaven compared to the mundane tedium of having to act nice.

LUCY KELLAWAY is a columnist on the Financial Times. *Her new novel,* In Office Hours, *is published by Penguin.*

Portrait of a Marriage

by SANDRINE BOYD

The National Gallery early on a Sunday morning: a place of echoing corridors and treasure hunts. But among the many paintings that have now become familiar friends, there is one that stands out for me: Jan van Eyck's *The Arnolfini Portrait*.

This wooden panel is my version of C. S. Lewis's wardrobe, opening a door to a world of faultless fantasy. I got married a year ago and van Eyck's painting embodies how I imagine a perfect marriage to be. It portrays the happiness and stability of a loving relationship. I don't worry too much about the complex iconography. I just let the forms and symbols construct their meaning and talk to me.

So few works of art can be relevant to the past, the present and the future. This, however, is eternity in a painting. Sometimes, I have to confess, I get frustrated. How am I supposed to achieve such an ideal state of marital bliss? An 'At Home with the Arnolfinis' magazine feature would doubtless show Mrs Arnolfini giving tips on how to run a tightly managed household while looking fabulous for her husband in an absurdly impractical gown. And that little dog would do Andrew Lloyd Webber proud as Toto in his upcoming *Wizard of Oz* production. It runs the risk of all looking a little smug.

But then it's also how I would like my home to look and feel – a welcoming, glossy bubble of perfection, far from the traffic frenzy and pigeons only a few yards away.

✎ SANDRINE BOYD *is an art historian who lives in London and is currently juggling writing her first novel and searching for a whippet puppy.*

Lonely as a Cloud

by JOHN SUTHERLAND

~

'I wandered lonely as a cloud,' wrote Wordsworth in his most famous spring lyric. Teachers often have to explain that, in this instance, 'loneliness' is good. Solitude (another favourite Wordsworthism) was, the poet believed, balm for the spirit.

Where, in today's teeming London, can one find and enjoy solitude? What little remains is a fast-vanishing commodity. The beautiful Gilbert Scott phone boxes – with their little zones of acoustic privacy – are going-gone. You must now phone in public to public annoyance.

'Public Conveniences' (delightful Victorian euphemism) are similarly disappearing – replaced, in areas where nocturnal alcohol consumption is high – by hideous plastic pissoirs with even less intimate coverage than their French originals.

There remain, thankfully, a few places where a Londoner like me can still find the kind of walkabout solitude Wordsworth needed for the health of his soul. Most satisfactorily Regent's Canal, between heaving King's Cross and sleepy Little Venice. On weekdays you can walk two miles along the old towpath, under dankly decaying bridges (some embellished with the solitary Banksy's artwork), and see no one other than the occasional gloomy angler and jogger. And this in the middle of a megalopolis of 11 million souls.

But what to do with that canal side loneliness? How to use it? There is a lesson to be found in the writings of the most heterodox novelist of our time, W. G. ('Max') Sebald. In *The Rings of Saturn*, burdened with a spiritual ailment he does not share with the reader, he records:

> In August 1992, when the dog days were drawing to an end, I set off to walk the county of Suffolk, in the hope of dispelling the emptiness that takes hold of me whenever I have completed a long stint of work.

It's not a holiday but spiritual repair Sebald had in mind. His solitary walk – not 'into' the county of Suffolk, but along its deserted pebbly rim, from Lowestoft to Felixstowe – was not, in the usual way, exploration, or tourism. His journey was, essentially, into his own mind. He needed loneliness for that.

A Catholic by birth, background and upbringing (in the foothills of the Alps) Sebald was practising the Ignatian exercise of meditation. It has a long history in literature, going back as far as the metaphysical poets. A familiar depiction shows a Jesuit priest gazing at a skull – his sole companion – on his desk. Sebald, as he tramps the beaches in *The Rings of Saturn*, contemplates (in his mind the skull of) his fellow East Anglian Sir Thomas Browne (author of the wonderful meditation, *Religio Medici*).

Meditation – something impossible to do in company – is an art we have lost. Life is too full, too busy; too much 'with us', as Wordsworth would say. We would be healthier if we recovered the skills of creative introspection and sought out, even in the most populous places of our country, the oases of loneliness – whether Lakeland, shingle strand, or the canal alongside the railway gasometers.

JOHN SUTHERLAND *is the emeritus Lord Northcliffe Professor at UCL, author of numerous books and a regular contributor to the* Guardian.

PART SEVEN

Final Thoughts

Meditation

by ANTHONY SELDON

I wouldn't have been concerned about happiness in my life if I hadn't, I think, been unhappy. Unhappiness and discontentment are powerful motivators towards the discovery of enduring happiness. Buddha and many other sages have long recognised this. My childhood was not any more happy or indeed unhappy I suspect than most, no doubt, but I found adolescence difficult, beset by doubts, fears and a sense that life had to be about more than the fraught existence I was living. University was chaotic, passed in a blur of directing plays, broken relationships, friends and sleepy forgetfulness.

Coming down to cold grey autumnal London from warm and glowing Oxford was a shock. On an Underground station one day, I saw a sign advertising the School of Meditation. 'Fed up with life, lows and lack of stability,' it said, or something like that. I decided to check it out, went to the introductory talk, signed myself up, and, hey presto, was 'initiated' into meditation in 1977 at the age of twenty-four. Shortly after, I began attending yoga classes at a 'squat' in Albany Street just off London's

Regent's Park. My life began to change. I gave up eating meat and drinking alcohol, spent part of the day on my head, and much of the rest of the day becoming what my friends saw, in one word, as 'strange'. Rather than inviting them to rock parties with endless Valpolicella and Soave, it was now about them bringing their favourite poem, piece of classical music, or moment of personal truth, and sharing them with everyone else to candlelight and joss sticks.

I loved much about this new life, but it was hard work, really hard work. Shortly after I began meditating, I spent five weeks in the US as part of my doctoral research, and my life simply fell apart. Was it because I had left behind the known signposts of my life for this new world of meditation and yoga? Quite possibly. I faced a life-changing decision. On the verge of breakdown, I had to decide should I abandon this new path, or continue with it, clinging tenaciously onto what felt like a life and death journey. I chose the path less travelled and gradually the fog began to lift and life became more secure, helped by meeting Joanna, who became my wife, and by settling down to a career in school teaching, the best profession under the sun.

Three or four years into the busy life of schools, I eventually began to move away from yoga and meditation. Work was simply too busy and the demands so great. The jitters and the jagged unpredictabilities of my late teens and early twenties had left me, and I saw no need to continue the austerities and disciplines of these Indian devices. Life took off. Three children suddenly pitched up on our sitting-room carpet in rapid succession in diapers, job promotions followed, books were written, and all seemed to be going fine.

But then, just after my fiftieth birthday, everything began unravelling. I no longer found meaning or security in the world I had constructed around me, and on a bleak holiday in Essaouira in Marrakesh I realised that life had to change. The essence is the switch to putting others rather than one's self at the heart of one's life. I started to meditate again, and went to Sivananda yoga ashrams in India and beyond. All very Spartan – up at 5.30 every morning, two meals a day, eight hours of yoga and silent reflection, and rest time cleaning out the toilets. After months of angst, my life began to clear again, but on a much deeper footing.

The journey is like falling awake, a steady movement towards reality and living in the present moment rather than a mental construction. You begin to see the world and people as they really are. I had always felt deeply religious, but I no longer felt the need to believe in any God or supernatural being: it is a matter simply of direct experience, of knowing that a silence beyond words is present and available every second of my life whenever I choose to turn to it. With Joanna and our children, the greatest source of happiness in my life, I am learning to accept them as they are, rather than as I might like them to be.

I have always loved the countryside, but now when I am in it, I can feel the wind, see the colours, and shapes, and smell the air, free of thoughts of past and future which so clouded my mind. I love nowhere more than where water and land meet, by rivers, lakes and the sea. This opaque mystical meeting point is like the congruousness of life and death, with boats havens of safety venturing out into those vast waters of the unknown, and encompassing one in a womb of safety.

With yoga comes a sense of extraordinary physical health and vitality, of intense life coursing through one's veins. I feel a sense of harmony and peace with my body, which helps me to feel at one with the world. I try to spend ten or fifteen minutes each day on yoga exercises, and to sit down for thirty minutes in the morning and the evening to meditate on my soft Sanskrit mantra.

Even if my material world becomes tempting and compelling again, as it did in my thirties and forties, it will never again cause me to abandon my connection to this deeper way of living. I do miss my Morgan sports cars with the aero screens, wooden dashboard and deep growl, Puligny Montratchet and steak mignon. There is nothing at all wrong with the pleasures of life, but they are always transitory, they always cost money and they are always egotistical experiences.

Most exciting of all is the sense I have that the happiness and joy I experience are only just the tip of the iceberg. They cost nothing, harm nobody and I feel connected to life in all its fullness. The future promise is that the joy will only get deeper year by year, and the fear of crossing that divide from dry land into the water, from life into death, fades into utter inconsequence.

❧ ANTHONY SELDON *is an authority on contemporary British history and headmaster of Wellington College. He is also the author or editor of over twenty-five works on contemporary history, politics and education. His latest books are* Trust: How We Lost It and How to Get It Back *and* Brown at 10.

The Gratitude Diaries
by SUE CREWE

One day, my heirs and successors will have to deal with my diaries. These volumes already occupy several feet of bookshelf and may have colonised several more by the time I'm done. They will notice that the A5 notebooks are in chronological order and that there is an entry for every day of the year. Already anachronistic – handwritten copy between hard covers – such a thing will be really quaint and bizarre in a couple of decades. Despite this, the heirs may be hopeful that they have come across a sensational cache of information and revelation.

Disappointingly for them, they will soon realise that there have never been such dull diaries. They contain no gossip or spicy anecdotes, they aren't written to entertain or even to provide a record of events: they are just an endless list of positives with not a bad word for anyone or anything. The heirs might well wonder why anyone would bother with such banalities as they pile the diaries into a skip; but what they couldn't know is that, within those pages, there is my not-so-secret formula for happiness.

Some years ago, after a period of turbulence in my life,

a friend introduced me to the concept of keeping 'a journal of gratitude'. She gave me the book in which it was to be kept and suggested how to use it. 'Every day find five things to be grateful for and write them down,' she instructed. The journal she'd given me only provided five blank lines per day so there was no room for qualification or complaint. For the first few months I dutifully performed the ritual at night. Often I found it difficult to think of enough things and took refuge in being grateful for my comfortable bed or being warm or well fed. If the day had gone badly I could always be grateful that it had come to an end.

After a while it began to be easier to find legitimate entries, and occasionally I had a problem with what should be left out. Rather than a chore, the diary-keeping was becoming a pleasure and the journal itself became precious and it was the first thing that went into the suitcase if I was going to be away from home.

Almost imperceptibly, free-floating anxiety and feelings of discontent with myself and the world were replaced by contentment and a clearer understanding of what I found acceptable and unacceptable about my own and other people's behaviour. Keeping a gratitude diary didn't prevent me from being a flawed human being or crashing the car or having rows or being lazy or suffering loss, but it did – and does – help me keep things in perspective.

For five years I replaced that first diary with physically identical ones, with the same rather cringe-making suggestions and aphorisms at the top of the page and the restricted space for entries. It was only in the sixth year that I felt secure enough in the gratitude-habit to buy a blank notebook and to embark on free-range gratitude diary keeping. Although the formula is the same – no more and no less than five things for which I am grateful – the extra space allows for a bit more elaboration; or possibly waffle.

I look back over past volumes from time to time and, given the limitations imposed by the formula, it is still extraordinary what a flood of recollection each page provokes. Some of them are extremely frustrating, for example one entry reads, 'I'm grateful that the chancellor agreed to the breakfast.' What was that about, I wonder, but the diary doesn't relate and I can't remember. The entries for the births of my three grandchildren, however (at which I was present), are equally succinct but they prompt the most vivid and detailed recall.

The diaries spell out very clearly what gives me the most satisfaction and pleasure. By far and away the most constant refrain is gratitude for my family and friends, for meals eaten together, for conversations, laughter and love. Running a close second are the occasions when I feel I've done a good job of work or completed some neglected or onerous task. Natural beauty and cerebral and sensory pleasures feature, but luxuries, possessions and treats hardly get a look in.

It's hard to maintain many illusions about oneself in the face of so much detailed evidence. If I'd fondly imagined that I was a party girl with a passion for music and literature, these diaries would put me straight because they actually portray a family-oriented home-body with a puritanical work ethic who likes cooking and swimming. But the most transformative revelation is the power of the gratitude itself: it takes up so much room that everything corrosive and depressing is squeezed to the margins. It seems to push out resentment, fear, envy, self-pity and all the other ugly sentiments that bring you down, leaving room for serenity, contentment and optimism to take up residence. Tracking gratitude doesn't, however, make for a very thrilling diary.

SUE CREWE *has been Editor of* House & Garden *since 1994. She lives in London and Cumbria where her house is on the mouth of a river. She has an extended family.*